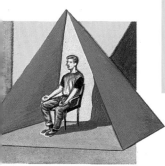

WORLD · MYSTERIES

THE

UNEXPLAINED

Pam Beasant

Illustrated by Tony Miller

Richard Draper, Anne Winterbotham and Paul Sullivan

Designed by Iain Ashman   Consultant Editor: Colin Wilson

Copy Editor: Stella Love   Picture Research: Constance Novis

CONTENTS

COLLINS

STRANGE DISAPPEARANCES

Every year, thousands of people go missing. Most of them either return or are found within a short time, but there are a few who, despite long searches for them, seem to have vanished off the face of the earth.

Some people, after careful planning, disappear on purpose. In order to escape problems, or even prison, they might change their name and appearance, and 'vanish' into another country. Others may disappear because they have lost their memory and cannot remember who they are or where they live. This condition is called amnesia, and usually happens as the result of a shock or a bang on the head.

In the strangest cases, neither planning nor amnesia can account for the disappearance of people in circumstances so odd that they defy natural explanation. In 1873, an English shoemaker called James Worson bet three friends that he could run all the way to Coventry and back; a distance of 25 kilometres. He set off with his friends following in a cart to make sure he did not cheat. Suddenly, before their eyes, he stumbled slightly and then vanished completely. Despite several searches, James Worson was never seen again.

Different beliefs

In the past, many people believed that those who vanished were taken by fairies. According to some *legends*,* fairies would steal a young baby and leave a fairy child, called a *changeling*, in its place. Now, however, some believe that people are whisked away by *aliens* in *UFOs*, and there are several stories on record from people who claim that they were picked up by aliens and examined before being returned to earth (see pages 14,15).

Some people also suggest that there are strong *force fields* in the world which, if walked through, can make people invisible for a while, or may even be doors to another world outside time and space.

In 1815, in Weichselmunde prison in Prussia, a prisoner called Diderici was walking in an exercise yard with other prisoners. Nobody could believe their eyes when Diderici suddenly began to fade. After a few seconds, he was completely invisible and his empty chains fell to the ground.

In 1872, a Mississippi riverboat, called 'Iron Mountain', left Vicksburg, USA, with 52 passengers and towing barges full of cotton and molasses. Not long after, another riverboat almost collided with the barges which had been cut from the 'Iron Mountain' and were drifting away. It was later discovered that the 'Iron Mountain', along with her crew, had vanished from the river without a trace. Nobody ever found wreckage, bodies or floating cargo, and the incident remains a mystery.

* Words appearing in italics are explained in the Glossary on pages 46-47.

In 1847, an explorer called Ludwig Leichardt led an expedition into the Australian Central Desert. Despite many searches for them, every member of the party vanished without trace, including 20 mules, 7 horses, 50 bullocks, and all their possessions.

Teleportation

Some people have vanished only to reappear miles away within a few seconds. This lightning method of travel is called *teleportation*, and it is believed to be controlled by the mind. In 1952, an Englishman called Wellesley Tudor Pole, arrived at the station which was 20 minutes walk from his home. It was 5.55 pm and at 6.00 pm he was expecting an important telephone call. He was desperate to find a way to get home on time. Suddenly, he was standing in his own hall just as the clock was striking six. He could offer no explanation for his experience except teleportation.

The 'Mary Celeste'

One of the most famous cases of disappearance happened in 1872, when the American ship 'Mary Celeste' was found deserted and drifting, but undamaged. The captain, Benjamin Briggs, who was sailing with his family and seven crew members, had obviously abandoned ship in a hurry as no personal possessions had been taken, with everything left as it was. A bed was found unmade, with a child's impression clearly visible. A blood-stained sword was found under the captain's bed, and when the ship was sailed to Gibraltar for inspection, some thought that the captain had been murdered by the crew who had then made their escape. The most likely theory, however, seems to be that the ship was hit by a *waterspout*, and they abandoned ship believing that she was more seriously damaged than she was. Nobody will ever know exactly what happened on board the 'Mary Celeste'; a ship which had always been dogged by bad luck.

The Philadelphia Experiment

It is claimed that in 1943, the US Navy made a top-secret experiment in which a ship, the 'USS Eldridge', vanished for a few minutes in the Philadelphia Navy Yard. Apparently, a strong force field was generated around the ship, which shimmered in a foggy green mist before disappearing. It is said that the crew suffered terrible after-effects from the experiment, such as burns and even madness. The US Navy denies ever making the experiment but it is a strange story for witnesses to have made up.

In December 1900, on the Scottish island Eilean Mor, the lighthouse was dark for 11 days. When the ship carrying supplies to the lighthouse arrived, it was discovered that the three keepers had vanished, leaving behind their oilskins. The lighthouse was in good order and there was no clue as to what had happened.

This map shows the general area of the Bermuda Triangle, where dozens of ships and aeroplanes have disappeared without trace. Some believe the area to be bigger than the triangle shows, and a different shape. The region has also been called the 'Limbo of the Lost', the 'Devil's Triangle', and the 'Magic Rhombus'.

In 1609, a British galleon, the 'Sea Venture' was wrecked off the coast of Bermuda on her way to America carrying a group of immigrants. The night before she reached Bermuda, a bright, star-like light had been seen dancing around on the ship, from sail to sail up and down the mainyard. The light apparently stayed with the ship half the night.

BERMUDA TRIANGLE

The 'Bermuda Triangle' is a large area, roughly in the shape of a triangle, lying between Florida, Puerto Rico and Bermuda. The area has gained its sinister reputation because of the number of ships and planes that have vanished there with no trace of bodies or wreckage.

The first person to report strange events in the Bermuda Triangle was Christopher Columbus, who sailed to America in 1492 from the Canary Islands. He described how his compass failed to function properly, and how he saw a strange fireball landing in the sea. He also saw an odd, bright glow on the horizon – a sight which has been reported by other people who have sailed through the area.

Flight 19

On 15th December, 1945, five US Navy Avenger bombers took off from Fort Lauderdale in Florida for what should have been a short routine patrol flight over the Atlantic. The weather was clear and warm, but after about two hours in the air, there was an emergency radio message from the Flight Leader, Charles Taylor, stating that Flight 19 was off course and they could not see any land. They were told to head West by the control tower, but Taylor replied that they no longer knew which way was West and everything looked strange. After that, radio contact became very bad and one of the pilots was heard to say that his instruments had all gone haywire. About two and a half hours later, a rescue team in a flying-boat set off with a crew of 13 on board. Neither the flying-boat nor the five bombers were ever seen again. It seems certain that they ran out of fuel, had to ditch in the sea and were drowned. What remains a complete mystery is why all six aircraft should have become lost and disorientated in the first place. The authorities maintained that the episode was a tragic accident, but it heralded the beginning of a spate of modern disappearances which labelled the area a danger zone.

Strange tales from the Triangle

As well as those who have vanished in the Bermuda Triangle, there are many who have survived odd, and sometimes frightening experiences there. They describe, for instance, how the radio went dead, the compass needle began to spin, or electrical power failed. Some

On the 5th December, 1945, five US Navy Avenger torpedo-bombers disappeared in the Bermuda Triangle while on a routine training flight. A Martin Mariner flying-boat which set o to rescue the Navy planes also vanished without trace that da (see main text).

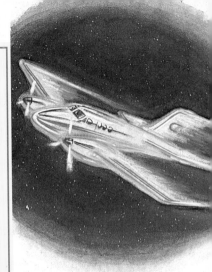

have also seen clouds or fog of yellow and green, in which the sea is very turbulent, no matter what the weather is like.

In 1974, a typical incident was reported. It concerned the liner QE2 which, when sailing through the area experienced extensive electrical and mechanical failure, including all the boilers which suddenly stopped working. The QE2 was being tracked on *radar* by a nearby Coast Guard boat, but it totally vanished from the screen during the power failures, although the crew on the deck of the boat could see the liner clearly.

Theories and explanations

Many people think that the Bermuda Triangle's reputation has been exaggerated and that the evidence for so many mysterious disappearances is not very strong. They say that many factors could account for the 'accidents', such as frequent and sudden storms, and a particularly fast-moving current that could carry unwary ships off course (although this does not account for the experience of those in aeroplanes). There are also pirates around the Caribbean who attack and steal small boats, mainly for the purpose of drug-smuggling.

Despite all these factors, however, there are still many convinced that there is something very odd about the area – and some even odder theories about it! Some believe that *aliens* who are studying our planet occasionally make off with human samples (See pages 14,15). Others think that it is a door into time, or a fourth dimension, through which one may travel to new worlds or into the future or the past.

A researcher called Ivan Sanderson claimed to have found 12 similar 'lozenge-shaped' regions worldwide, which he called 'vile vortices'. One off the coast of Japan, known as the Devil's Sea, was declared a danger zone in 1955 by the Japanese authorities after many vessels had vanished there over a period of several years. Sanderson believed that disturbance in these areas is related to earthquakes and caused by whirlpools started by activity in the earth's crust. It is also believed that it is caused by bursts of magnetic activity in the earth's molten iron core. This would explain spinning compasses and loss of electrical power. Until there is a complete study of the *phenomena*, however, the mystery of the Bermuda Triangle remains.

In 1964, Chuck Wakely, a charter pilot on his way to Florida, suddenly noticed a strange glow around the wings of his aeroplane while at an altitude of 2000 metres. The glow gradually became brighter and brighter and the electronic equipment failed leaving Wakely with only manual control. Eventually the glow began to fade and the instruments returned to normal.

In 1955, the ship 'Atlantic City', which was on automatic steering as she went through the Triangle, suddenly began to steer in a circle and the compass and electrical equipment failed. A lookout on board later described a large ball of fire that he had seen passing overhead at the same time.

Prehistoric monuments, such as standing stones and earthen burial mounds, are thought to have been deliberately built where two or more lines of magnetic force in the earth, ley lines, cross and the force is strongest. It is thought that the stones were used to tap this force and use its energy.

FORCES FROM THE EARTH

In 1921, a man called Alfred Watkins noticed that many *standing stones*, ancient churches and burial mounds line up with each other. He was the first to suggest that the straight lines which ran between them were ancient pathways, and the monuments marked out the paths across the countryside. Watkins called these paths *'ley lines'*. Later, it was thought that ley lines were not paths on the surface of the earth, but were actually lines of magnetic force that ran under the earth. Now, many think that ancient man knew about this force, and deliberately built monuments and burial places where the force seemed strongest. They then used the force in special religious rituals to 're-charge' themselves.

Ley lines and dowsing

Dowsing is the ability to find substances such as water or minerals hidden underground using a dowsing rod or pendulum which will twist or swing in the dowser's hands when the substance is located. It is not known why dowsing works. Many think that the dowser's muscles unconsciously react to changes in the earth's magnetic field, which are caused by the hidden substance, and this causes the rod to twist or pendulum to swing.

Most dowsers are convinced that ley lines exist and can be traced with a dowsing rod. Some, who dowse near standing stones or other ancient monuments, are knocked down by the force they feel from them. One dowser, Bill Lewis, who carried out a dowsing experiment at a standing stone, found that the magnetic force went round the stone in a spiral.

Dragon paths

The Chinese have always recognized lines of force in the earth. They call them dragon paths, or 'lung-mei', and the art of tracing them out, 'feng-shui', was a very important and ancient skill. It was forbidden to build on an imperial dragon path, and even the Emperors, who were regarded as gods, would not build a palace or a tomb without taking advice about dragon paths. One young man who was accidentally buried on a dragon path, was ordered to be dug up and moved. In Chinese tradition, the dragon is the link between earth and sky, and the paths are the routes along which the

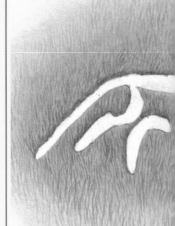

Ley lines are sometimes thought to form animal shapes on the countryside, English hill figures, such as the white horse in Uffington, Wiltshire, traced out by ancient man, are thought to

It is claimed that *supernatural* events occur at the point where two or more ley lines cross. One researcher, Stephen Jenkins, twice saw phantom soldiers at the same spot in Cornwall, England. The soldiers, all armed, were silent and still. They

have been drawn using the ley lines as a guide. The eye of the horse is supposed to lie right over a specially powerful part of the ley line called a blind spring.

vanished completely after a curtain of hot air seemed to waver around them. Jenkins believes that the ley lines triggered off a powerful *force field*. The two sightings occurred 40 years apart.

dragon travels. The dragon itself is a symbol of luck and power.

Fairy paths

In Ireland and Brittany, France, the lines of force are called fairy paths. They run in straight lines between ancient hill forts which were traditionally thought of as fairy fortress. The fairy paths in Ireland are never built on and are avoided on certain days of the year on which it is believed that the fairies have their processions. In 1935, an Irishman called Michael O'Hagan, built an extension on his house which blocked a fairy path. One by one, his five children fell mysteriously ill, and remained so until the extension was demolished and the fairy path clear again.

Ghosts and UFOs

All sorts of strange *phenomena* are associated with ley lines. For instance, ghosts and *UFOs* are often seen on or near them and some believe that UFOs use them for navigation. The point where two or more ley lines cross is said to be especially powerful. One researcher, Tom Lethbridge, believed that these points may act like 'trapdoors' into another world which is parallel to ours but has different laws of time and space.

Another strange phenomenon that occurs on ley lines is the appearance of huge phantom black dogs (called Cu sith in Scotland). The dogs always follow the same route and are thought of as an *omen* of death if seen. One is supposed to run from an ancient church through a village in Devonshire, England. It makes a terrible noise as it goes, sounding as if it is causing extensive damage, although no harm ever comes to people or buildings.

'Living' stones

Some people think that strange earth forces such as those that create ley lines, account for the many reports and *legends* about stones that seem to be alive. According to some, there are stones which move, grow, and even generate new stones. The Rollright Stones in Oxfordshire, England, are believed to move to nearby water for a 'drink' on the same day every year. One of them, 'the King's Stone' always moves back to where it was if moved by anyone. Many researchers dismiss such stories as nonsense, although there are some who believe that there is still much we do not know about forces that could cause such phenomena.

Disaster is supposed to befall any who obstruct fairy paths in Ireland. The owner of this cottage cut off the corner after discovering it jutted into a fairy path. The disturbances which had been bothering the family, stopped straight away.

Death Valley, in California, USA, is said to contain stones that move mysteriously by themselves. No one ever sees them move, but they go in all directions and slide rather than roll. In the 1970s, one large stone apparently moved 64 metres. Theories about the moving stones range from moon influence to UFO interference, but the mystery has never been solved.

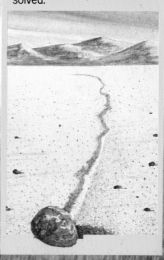

Pyramids have been built by ancient man all over the world, not just in Egypt, although none are as impressive as the Egyptian ones. Some, however, are very strange indeed. One in the Himalayan mountains in Tibet is reportedly made of shimmering white material with a strange crystal shining on top. It was apparently seen from an aeroplane and photographs of it mysteriously disappeared later. Many doubt the existence of this pyramid.

PYRAMID POWER

There are about 80 pyramids in Egypt which stand as monuments to the ancient Egyptians who built them almost 5,000 years ago. Although some of them are little more than ruins, they still show the amazing skill and workmanship of the Egyptian engineers and labourers. Even today, with modern equipment, it would take six years to build a copy of the largest pyramid, and cost one billion dollars. *Mummified* remains have been found in some of the pyramids, and experts believe that they were built as tombs for the pharaohs (kings) or as temples to the Egyptian gods. This has never been proved, however, and some suggest that they are libraries that record the history of ancient man. This is because ancient Egyptian hieroglyphics, a form of picture writing, have been found all round the walls of the chambers inside the pyramids. Some think that the pyramids also predict future events, including the end of the world.

Preserving powers

Whatever the reason for their building, many acknowledge that the pyramids have strange powers. A French researcher, Antoine Bovis, discovered preserved dogs, cats and other animals in the Great Pyramid at Giza, near Cairo. After doing several experiments preserving fresh food such as meat and eggs in scale models of the Great Pyramid, Bovis realized that there was a connection between its shape, the position of the animals, and its preserving power. (Some people now use model pyramids to store fresh foods, and in some countries, milk is sold in pyramid containers.)

Sharpening razors

A Czechoslovakian radio technician, Karl Dbarl, read about Bovis's experiments and tried them himself. He experimented further and found out that a pyramid would also keep razor blades sharp, and restore blunt ones to good working order. His experiments worked in pyramids of any shape and size, not just a scale model of the Great Pyramid, although this seemed to be best. Dbarl designed a razor-sharpener which has been produced and sold successfully ever since. He never found out exactly why it worked, but believes it is a combination of energy from the sun and energy from the earth which is concentrated

The Great Pyramid was built by the pharaoh Cheops, at Giza, near Cairo. Originally it was 146 metres high, but has since been worn down to 137 metres. It is made from 2,500,000 blocks of limestone each weighing between 2 and 15 tonnes. A workforce of 4000-10,000 men took 20-30 years to build it, with extra labour being drafted in over the summer. With its complex network of tunnels and chambers, it is the most impressive and studied of the pyramids. Strange powers are attributed to it which can be duplicated in scale models (see main text).

by the pyramid shape into a powerful force. This force preserves materials by drying them out and killing the germs that cause rot, or in the case of the razor blades, it rearranges the particles in the edge of the blade, 'stretching' them back into shape.

Other powers of the pyramids

Many think that pyramids have other, stranger, powers. People who are *psychic* have claimed that a pyramid can improve their powers of communication with the spirits and other mental powers such as *telepathy* and *psychokinesis* (moving objects through thought power, without touching them.) Others think that sleeping with a pyramid under the bed ensures a clear head in the morning and fills one with energy. Those who *meditate* sometimes use pyramids as they say it concentrates the mind very well. Some people have built their own pyramids which they use to increase their energy level when required. Others have had pyramid-shaped houses built. There are also office blocks, restaurants and churches amongst other public buildings that have been built as pyramids. No one has yet surveyed the people who use these buildings to see if they notice any advantages.

Inside the Great Pyramid

One researcher, Dr Paul Brunton, decided to spend the night inside the Great Pyramid of Giza, to see if he had any unusual experiences. He fasted for three days beforehand so that his mind would be more receptive to any 'psychic energy' Dr Brunton stayed in the King's Chamber (where the preserved animals were found). He noticed immediately that there was an eerie coldness that cut to his bones. As he sat in the dark, he felt an overwhelming bad presence and then claimed to see deformed spirits flitting around the chamber. Then, the atmosphere became friendly and two figures appeared which looked like ancient Egyptian high priests. Brunton had the strange feeling of leaving his body and floating round the chamber. One priest then told him to tell people to stop going to war and ignoring the Creator, or they would be destroyed. Dr Brunton's experience may have been a vivid dream, but the accounts of other people of strange 'atmospheres' inside the pyramids, convince many that they do have powers that may not yet be understood.

One strange property of pyramids is that they seem to accumulate static electricity. A British inventor noticed that his fingers prickled if he raised them on top of the Great Pyramid. Using a bottle wrapped in wet newspaper as a rechargeable 'battery', he held it above his head until sparks literally flew off it. A guide accidentally touched by the bottle received a terrible electric shock.

Besides their preserving and sharpening powers, pyramids are thought to have healing properties. Some people sit in large pyramids to relieve the pain of arthritis or rheumatism. People sometimes find that by placing a pyramid underneath their bed or chair so that it is directly beneath the pain, the pain is quickly relieved. Some also wear pyramid hats to get rid of headaches.

In June, 1954, a woman in Birmingham, England, was caught in a storm with her son and daughter on the way to a fair. They heard thudding noises on the little girl's umbrella, and looking round, they realized that hundreds of tiny frogs were pouring down from the sky.

Thousands of snakes fell over part of Memphis, Tennessee, in 1877. They all measured between 30 and 45 centimetres, and were alive and apparently unharmed by their fall.

AMAZING RAIN

Although we know a good deal about our skies, and experts can predict most kinds of weather, there is still no explanation for the strange showers of objects and animals which have been reported all over the world. Through the centuries, people have been pelted from the sky by all manner of things such as; frogs, fish, snakes, fruit, nuts and even money. These amazing showers can last from a few minutes to several hours and they do not seem to be linked with any particular weather. They are equally likely to fall from clear skies as during a storm along with ordinary rain. In some cases it has been noticed that small clouds of various colour; usually red, green, yellow or black, have been hovering during the strange downpour.

Expecting the unexpected

In Honduras, Central America, a deluge of sardines falls at the beginning of the rainy season every year. The people are now so used to the shower that they lay out buckets and nets to catch the fish to eat.

Tornadoes and waterspouts

Many people think that *tornadoes* and *waterspouts* are responsible for all strange showers reported. Both will suck up anything in their path and could easily carry light creatures such as frogs and fish for miles. The theory does not explain, however, why a shower of frogs deposited by a tornado should contain only frogs and not other debris, such as mud, stones, fence-posts or other small animals. It also does not explain why so many creatures are alive when they reach the ground; the force and shock of a tornado should kill them. Also, a tornado moves quickly over the ground and does not hover in one place, yet strange showers are often repeated at the same spot, either within a few hours, or sometimes days, of the first.

Aliens and poltergeists

Some believe that the creatures and objects that fall from the sky have been released by *UFOs*, and were collected as samples from earth to study. Others think that there are invisible worlds which exist alongside our own, and the skyfall consists of things which have somehow moved through a

In July, 1827, half a ton of hay was seen flying overhead against the wind by field-workers in Denbighshire, Wales. As the hay went past, a few strands floated down on the surprised workers.

During a storm in August, 1940, hundreds of silver coins fell over the Central Russian region of Meshchera. Similar rains of money have been reported in France and Germany.

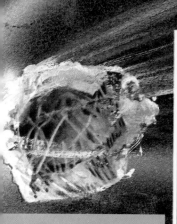

A gopher turtle, encased in ice, fell over Mississippi, USA, in 1894 during a bad hailstorm. (The year before, an alligator dropped on Charleston, USA.)

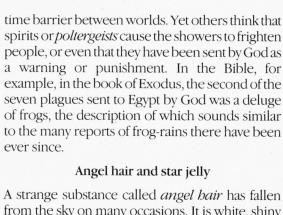

time barrier between worlds. Yet others think that spirits or *poltergeists* cause the showers to frighten people, or even that they have been sent by God as a warning or punishment. In the Bible, for example, in the book of Exodus, the second of the seven plagues sent to Egypt by God was a deluge of frogs, the description of which sounds similar to the many reports of frog-rains there have been ever since.

Angel hair and star jelly

A strange substance called *angel hair* has fallen from the sky on many occasions. It is white, shiny and thread-like, said to be like silk, cotton wool or spiders' webs. In one case, a ship moored in her berth, became totally draped with white threads which were falling from the sky. When the captain picked up some of the threads to examine them, they felt strong, but disintegrated after lying in his hand for a few minutes. In many UFO sightings, angel hair has also been seen. In 1948, in Ontario, Canada, a man saw many bright spheres travelling across a clear sky and trailing white threads which were each about three or four metres long.

This vanishing quality of angel hair also applies to a slimy substance called *star jelly* which, in the past, was believed to mark the place where a star fell, or a *meteorite* landed on earth. Now, however, it is thought to be simply a type of fungus, or a mass of insect eggs, although it disintegrates before it can be properly analysed. In 1883, in New Jersey, USA, fiery rain poured out of the sky. When witnesses arrived at the place, they found lumps of star jelly. A transparent jelly-like mass also fell right beside a woman milking a cow nearby, but when others came to see it, only a few white particles remained.

Charles Fort

Much of our knowledge about strange skyfalls is due to an American called Charles Fort, who was born in New York in 1874. He spent nearly 25 years scanning old, forgotten documents and newspapers in libraries and museums for unusual stories which he then put together in a series of best-selling books. He aimed to prove that the world was much more mysterious than scientists allow it to be.

In 1968, it was reported that a carpenter had been impaled and killed by a huge icicle as he worked on a roof in Kempten, W. Germany. The icicle was apparently 1.80 metres long, and 15 centimetres wide.

In 1578, large, yellow mice were reported to have fallen over Bergen in Norway. The very next year, there was a fall of lemmings in the same place.

On August 12th, 1883, a Mexican astronomer, José Bonilla, saw 283 UFOs through his telescope in the space of two hours. The objects were small, *luminous*, and gave out long trains of light. They passed in front of the sun in small groups. The next morning, Bonilla saw 116 more of the objects. He took photographs of what he saw and thought the UFOs were travelling somewhere between the earth and the moon.

A Swedish couple, on holiday in Gotland, saw a disc-shaped object flying in from the sea. It made two sharp turns before disappearing. Another object appeared and followed the same course. Both were silver and had riveted joints on the bottom. The upper section rotated on the lower, and the objects made a clicking sound. Both had a red tube and were fuzzy round the edges. They flew so low that tree-tops swayed and water rippled as they passed.

INTRODUCTION TO UFOs

The biggest mystery this century has been the thousands of reports from all over the world of unidentified flying objects, or *UFOs*. Many sightings turn out to be something ordinary, such as an airborne device to monitor the weather, or even a natural *phenomenon* such as a *meteorite* or *ball lightning*. There remain, however, truly unknown objects which have baffled scientists and led to the belief that we are visited by technologically superior *aliens* from other planets. Some people claim to have seen UFOs on the ground, and strange *humanoid* figures emerging from them. Some even say that they have been captured by aliens and taken away for examination before being dumped back on earth (see pages 14,15).

UFOs have been seen at all times of the day and night, and are a variety of shapes and sizes. They usually travel very quickly and perform amazing aerobatics such as right-angled turns at speeds of up to 18,000 kilometres per hour. This is impossible for any known aeroplane, apart from the fact that the air resistance would cause the aeroplane to burn up at that speed. Also, a human pilot would be unable to cope with the great forces such speed would produce.

What UFOs look like

One of the odd things about UFO reports is the similarity between them. The objects are often described as disc-shaped, and a common description of them is that they are like two dishes stuck together. Another common shape is long and thin, like a rocket or a cigar, with no fins or wings of any kind. These UFOs are usually very large, and are referred to as 'mother-ships', because they are often seen accompanied by a fleet of small discs.

UFOs are usually metallic and smooth with a row of windows like an aeroplane. They fly noiselessly and appear to change colour as they move, sometimes glowing red as they accelerate.

Kenneth Arnold's sighting

In 1947, an American businessman, Kenneth Arnold, took off in his private aeroplane to search for the remains of a crashed aeroplane on Mount

In 1954, a Boeing Stratocruiser airliner, on its way from New York to London, saw seven UFOs as they flew over Labrador. One was big and bright, and appeared to change shape as it flew along parallel to the airliner. The other six were small and appeared to be following the large one's lead. The UFOs travelled alongside the airliner for 18 minutes before the small ones began to disappear, as if inside the large one. Finally, the large object flew off very fast.

Rainier in Washington State. As he was flying over the mountain, he suddenly saw nine shiny discs travelling at more than 1500 kilometres an hour – a speed which no aeroplane could manage at that time. The discs wove in and out of the mountain tops, travelling in close formation like geese, and flying bumpily, like stones being skimmed across water. Arnold likened the aircraft to flying saucers, a description which was repeated in the press and has stuck ever since. This sighting, which received wide publicity, marked the beginning of the modern interest in UFOs. It was to be followed by thousands of similar sightings reported in regional and national newspapers around the world.

The 'Foo-Fighters'

Near the end of the Second World War (1939-1945), Japanese, German, American and British bomber-crews were sometimes tailed by strange glowing lights on their night-time bombing missions. The lights were red, orange or white balls, which would always soar up behind the bombers, then level off and follow for a while before turning and whizzing off again. Witnesses were always struck by how the balls seemed to be driven and steered rather than move randomly. At the time, each crew thought the balls were secret enemy weapons, and it was not until later that it was discovered that each country was as baffled as the next. After the War, the balls were nick-named 'foo-fighters' after a popular saying of an American comic-strip character.

Early UFO sightings

Although most UFO sightings have been reported this century, descriptions by ancient historians of strange objects in the sky sometimes sound just like the modern UFO reports. There are also tantalizing hints, such as the rock-drawings found on a Chinese island, dated nearly 47,000 years ago, which seem to depict cigar-shaped UFOs with alien occupants.

An historian, Conrad Wolffhart, recorded that in AD 393, a bright globe appeared in the sky one night. Later, other, smaller globes were seen flying towards it. For a while, they wheeled about, their lights dazzling to the eye, and then they gathered into a formation like a two-edged sword and their bright lights appeared as one flame. This account resembles the sightings of small disc-shaped UFOs flying in formation with a cigar-shaped 'mother-ship'.

One September night in 1976, the people of Teheran, Iran, reported a strange light in the sky. An F-4 jet, sent up to investigate, lost all power. A second F-4 approached cautiously but had to dive when a small bright object was fired from the UFO. The F-4's weapon power failed and the object tailed the jet for a while before returning to the larger ship. A second object was seen to shoot from the UFO and land softly on earth. The whole incident remains unexplained.

On 31st December, 1978 an Australian TV crew flying near New Zealand's South Island filmed a bell-shaped object with a bright base and transparent dome. It was tracked on *radar*, both in the aeroplane and on the ground, which showed more objects nearby. Later pictures showed one doing a figure-8 loop at 5000 kilometres per hour. No expert has ever explained these pictures and they remain very convincing evidence for UFOs.

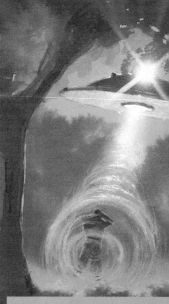

A 'Close Encounter of the First Kind' happened in Ohio, USA, in 1966. Just before daybreak two policemen saw a UFO flying low towards them. It hovered overhead, humming all the time and was so bright they had to look away. As it moved off, they chased it in their car. Seventy kilometres later they met another policeman who was also in pursuit. After another 70 kilometres they met yet another policeman standing by the road observing the object. All the policemen later gave statements that matched exactly. The object was 7.50-9 metres in diameter.

'CLOSE ENCOUNTERS'

The phrase *'Close Encounter'* was coined by an American scientist, Dr J. Allen Hynek, who worked for years on 'Project Blue Book', a research body sponsored by the US Air Force to investigate *UFO* reports. Dr Hynek categorized all UFO sightings closer than 150 metres into groups called Close Encounters of the First, Second and Third kinds. The first applies to sightings in which there is no interaction between the UFO and the environment. The second is when the UFO leaves traces such as burn marks on the ground. A Close Encounter of the third kind is when people have some contact with the occupants of the UFOs. A fourth kind of Close Encounter is now recognized in which people have contact with *aliens* inside UFOs. Those who claim to have been kidnapped by UFOs fall into this last group.

Close Encounters of the Second Kind

Those who think of UFOs as figments of the imagination find it hard to explain the occasions on which traces of the UFO 'visit' are left. The most common of these are flattened vegetation, scorch marks on the ground and radiation in soil and plants which is found on analysis. Another common UFO interference is engine failure in cars and aeroplanes and electronic failure of all kinds near a UFO. In 1957, for instance, a lorry driver on a Texas highway, saw what looked like a big flame ahead of him. When it was overhead, his lights and engine stopped working. The driver later said that the object looked like a 60-metre long torpedo and moved about 1000-1300 kilometres per hour. Other eye-witnesses later confirmed this description.

In 1972, puzzling marks were found in the Transylvanian Alps in Rumania after an old man saw a strange object land the night before. A ring 6 metres in diameter of flattened cornstalks was found in a field, in the middle of which was a 2.50-metre hole bored into the earth. Round the edge of the hole were three marks as if from stabilising 'feet'. Samples from the area showed a high level of radiation, and the grass was scorched. Also, moles there were coming out of hibernation early, as if they had been exposed to heat.

In 1952, a scoutmaster called C. Desverges had a 'Close Encounter of the Second Kind' in Florida, USA, while driving scouts home. He stopped to investigate a light in a thicket and as he made his way into it, he noticed a strong smell, and it became hot. He looked up and saw a large, dark object hovering 9 metres above him. It was

In 1954, two lorry drivers had a frightening 'Close Encounter of the Third Kind' in Caracas, Venezuela. When they stopped to investigate a strange object hovering above the road ahead, one of the drivers was attacked by a hairy dwarf-like creature with glowing eyes and sharp claws. He was light but very

Close Encounters of the Third Kind

In 1961, in Wisconsin, USA, Joe Simonton watched a silvery UFO land in his back garden. He approached the craft and was alarmed when three figures emerged from a hatch. They were about 1.30 metres tall and had dark hair and skin. One gave Simonton a jug, indicating that he wanted water. They then proceeded to cook dry pancake-like objects on a flameless stove. Before they left, they gave four of them to Simonton, one of which he ate although it apparently tasted like cardboard. When another pancake was analysed, it contained flour, sugar and fat – hardly very alien ingredients although Simonton swears that the story is true.

Not all aliens, however, seem so friendly. In 1952, a group of people went to a hillside in West Virginia, USA, to investigate what they thought was a crashed *meteorite*. Instead, however, the whole group saw a large globe which made a throbbing noise. In a torch-beam, they also saw to their horror, a monstrous creature standing nearby. It was 3-4.50 metres tall, had a bright red face and green/orange, glowing eyes. It floated towards the terrified group who fled at once. Skid marks and flattened grass were later found in the area.

Close Encounters of the Fourth Kind

Those who scoff at the idea of seeing aliens emerging from UFOs are often baffled by people who claim to have been kidnapped by UFOs, or to have had prolonged close contact with aliens. Fantastic as the stories are, those who report them are often genuinely frightened or affected in some way by their experience. In some cases, there are even physical signs of contact that bear out the story. A Brazilian farmer called Antonio Villas Boas, claims that in 1957 an egg-shaped UFO landed in his field, causing his tractor engine to fail. He was taken inside the craft, where five *humanoid* figures were talking in a language that sounded like barking dogs. They wore helmets and overalls, had light eyes and were just over 1.50 metres tall. They stripped Boas and took a blood sample from his chin. Eventually, he was shown round the craft which he later described in great detail. When Boas was examined by doctors later, he was found to have an unusually high level of radiation. There were also two puncture marks on his chin from where he claims the blood sample was taken.

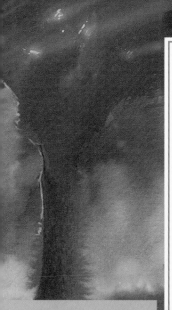

disc-shaped, grey and had a dome on top. Suddenly a small red ball appeared which turned into mist and enveloped him. The scouts in the car now ran for help. Later, flattened grass was found in the area, and Desverges noticed burns on his skin. Hairs on his arms were singed and his cap was charred.

strong, and threw the driver 4.50 metres. As they fought, a second creature blinded him with a light in a small tube. Meanwhile, the second driver saw that two more were going back inside the UFO carrying rocks and earth. Later, the first driver found a long, deep scratch on his side.

One of the classic 'Close Encounters of the Fourth Kind' happened to Barney and Betty Hill in 1961 as they drove home from holiday. They stopped to look at a moving light in the sky, and the next thing they remember is driving around two hours later in a confused state. Under *hypnosis*, however, they both give an amazing account of how they were taken on board the UFO by eight or so uniformed 'men', where samples of hair, skin and nails were taken. The leader also showed Betty a 'star map' of where they came from, which she drew under hypnosis. Apparently it showed correct star data which were not known in 1961.

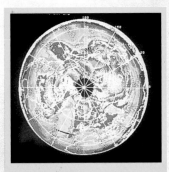

Those who believe that UFOs come from the centre of the earth, rather than outer space, claim that this photograph proves their theory by showing the entrance gap over the North Pole. In fact, the photograph was taken by a satellite over 24 hours, and the time lapse only gives the impression of a hole.

Many believe that we were visited thousands of years ago by alien astronauts who helped build monuments such as stone circles and the pyramids. It is thought that these acted as beacons for UFOs, guiding them in to land. Some rock carvings and inscriptions on tombs, which look rather like spacemen, have also been used as evidence of ancient astronauts.

UFO IDEAS AND EXPLANATIONS

There are about 200 billion stars in our *Milky Way* alone and some of these probably have planets which could support life. It seems likely that we are not alone in the Universe. While many scientists accept this, most are unwilling to believe that *aliens* in *UFOs* actually visit us regularly. For a start, we are right on the edge of the *Galaxy*, hundreds or thousands of light years away from other potential life sources. We only started signalling our existence by radio about thirty years ago, so it would be many years before an alien spacecraft would reach us, even if they had the technology to travel at the speed of light. The sheer number of UFO sightings also makes some scientists *sceptical* as they think it unlikely that, if aliens have found us accidentally, they should spend so much time and trouble on us. (By 1982, one UFO research centre in America had collected 70,000 sightings, 20% of which remain unexplained.) Many believe however, that UFOs are occupied by aliens and even if they are not, the question still remains: what are UFOs?

Different theories

One of the oddest theories about the occupants of UFOs is that they are bees from Mars! This is because it is thought that the complicated flying done by UFOs at high speeds could only be coped with by intelligent insects. Another theory is that the UFOs themselves are living alien animals. Again, this would account for their flying ability.

Some reject the idea of aliens altogether and think that UFOs are strange *phenomena* of this world. *Ball lightning*, for instance, which is a rare burst of lightning concentrated into a ball shape, could look like a flying saucer as it crosses the sky. Some of those who think that all UFOs are of this world also believe that they may be secret weapons being developed by one or other of the Super Powers. Given that many UFOs are openly seen over cities, however, this idea hardly seems likely.

Hidden civilizations?

In the 19th century a small group of people put forward the idea that the earth is hollow. They said it could be entered at either of the two poles, and contained beautiful worlds full of strange new peoples. In the 1960s, the hollow earth theory

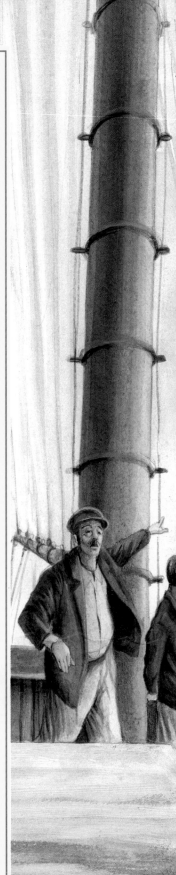

became popular again in connection with UFOs, as some believed that aliens came from 'inner' instead of 'outer' space. This belief still persists despite the fact that scientists have proved that the earth is solid.

Another popular belief is that UFOs come from cities under the water. Some think that legendary lost civilizations, such as Atlantis (see pages 40, 41) which supposedly destroyed itself with terrible weapons, are still alive deep under the ocean, and have developed amazing flying machines.

UFOs and ghosts

One of the most popular beliefs about UFOs is that they are similar to ghosts, and may exist in another dimension altogether. Some think there may be a parallel universe to our own, with different laws of time and space, which contains spirits which are sometimes visible to us, UFOs, like ghosts, are also often seen on the intersection of two or more *ley lines* (see pages 6, 7) which strengthens this connection.

Some go further and think that these 'spirits' are trying to gain control of our minds. This curious idea came about when odd things began to happen to some people seriously studying UFOs. Some, for instance, have seen 'men in black', who appear and disappear like ghosts and warn people to stop investigating UFOs without giving a reason. They seem to be able to read minds, see the future and always have an uncanny knowledge of the person they visit. One investigator, John Keel, went into a motel chosen at random only to find a message waiting for him at the desk.

Why should UFOs visit?

If UFOs do contain aliens from some other world, many people wonder why they visit as they never seem to make proper contact while here. In many alien sightings they have been described as gathering samples of earth and plants, presumably for analysis, and many of those who have been 'kidnapped' by aliens describe how they were examined. Some believe that aliens are only here to give us good advice; some have even had messages and warnings that we must live more peaceably with each other. Others think that aliens have a more sinister purpose and are here on a military-style reconnaissance to see how ripe we are to be taken over. Whatever their reasons, if aliens visit as often as it is claimed, they seem determined to keep their secrets.

In 1879, the crew of the ship 'Vulture' saw two huge glowing wheels spinning slowly into the Persian Gulf waters. Over the next few years, several other ships saw similar wheels in that part of the sea. These sightings fuelled the belief that UFOs came from under the water, perhaps from lost civilizations that had survived in some way.

In 1953, Albert Bender closed down the International Flying Saucer Bureau in Connecticut, USA because he claimed he was being plagued by strange 'men in black' who were warning him against investigating UFOs. The men, who had glowing eyes, apparently transported him to their base in Antarctica on one occasion.

In 1964, Gary Wilcox, a farmer in New York State, USA saw a strange egg-shaped object land in his field. Two hooded 'dwarfs' appeared carrying trays of seeds and other samples. They said they were from Mars, and took their food from the atmosphere which is why they were studying Earth farming methods. They asked for a bag of fertiliser so that night Wilcox left a bag out and the next day it was gone.

MAN-MADE ODDITIES

In many parts of the world, our ancestors left intricate and sometimes huge monuments some of which took hundreds of years to build and for which we no longer know the purpose. In some cases, it seems incredible that they were built at all, either because of their massive size, or their seeming uselessness.

In Mexico, for instance, when the ancient city of Monte Alban was *excavated* in the 1930s, a network of tiny, stone-lined tunnels was found running underneath the city. The first tunnel, explored in 1933, was only just large enough for the excavators to squeeze through lying on their backs. They found two skeletons in the tunnel, which had been buried with precious ornaments. Leading from the main tunnel, there were smaller tunnels, no more than 30 centimetres high, one of which had a tiny flight of steps leading down to it.

None of the experts could work out the purpose of these tunnels and having ruled out their use as drains or sewers, they remain to this day a mystery.

The Nazca lines of Peru

Some of the most breathtaking and puzzling monuments in the world can be found in Peru, on a plain that measures 320 square kilometres, near the town of Nazca. The works consist of hundreds of huge patterns, made from small stones. The amazing thing about the patterns is that they can only be seen from the air, although they are thought to have been made between 1,000 and 2,000 years ago – more than a thousand years before the first aeroplane flew. Some of the markings are simply straight lines while others show shapes such as triangles or spirals, and animals, birds and insects.

No one knows why the Nazca lines were made. Some *UFO* enthusiasts claim that they were built by *aliens* and used as runways for spacecraft. This would seem far-fetched, however, given that the lines are many kilometres long, and most UFOs are reported as landing vertically. One of the most popular theories is that they are some sort of calendar and observatory, as some lines seem to mark the winter and summer *solstices*, and the *equinoxes*. The most likely builders of the lines are the Nazca Indians who lived in the area but died out in the 16th century

All over North America, there are traces of forgotten peoples in the form of forts, cities, *standing stones* and tombs. Some of the most impressive of these monuments to early Americans are the Effigy Mounds, huge *earthmounds* in the shape of animals. One of them in Ohio is called the Great Serpent Mound and is 370 metres long. No one knows who built it or for what reason. American Indians say that the Effigy Mounds were already abandoned when their ancestors settled in America.

A white trident symbol overlooks Pisco Bay in Peru. It is 148 metres high, and carved out of stony salt which makes it shine white in the sun. Fishermen use it as a marker to guide them into the port. Some *UFOlogists* claim that the trident was carved by aliens to guide their spacecraft to Nazca, but it is more likely to be a sign to mark the *prehistoric* burial place that was excavated at the site.

This picture shows some of the Nazca lines in Peru. Thought by some to be giant runways for UFOs, their real purpose remains a mystery (see main text).

One of the most puzzling things about the Nazca lines is why they should have been made so intricately when the people had no way of viewing their work. In 1975, however, two researchers carried out an experiment. They built a hot-air balloon from materials the Nazcans were known to possess and successfully flew across the plain, showing that the Nazcans may have had this technology, and overseen the building of the lines in this way.

Noah's Ark

The story of the flood that wiped out every family in the world except one, is told and believed all over the world in different forms. In the Bible, Noah and his family are the ones who escape, taking with them two of every animal. The Ark that Noah built is still believed by many to be resting on Mount Ararat in Turkey where it was stranded when the level of the great flood waters fell. Over the years, there have been many expeditions to Mount Ararat in search of the Ark, and many people claim to have seen it, or bits of wood from it at least.

The most detailed account came from two Turkish journalists in 1949, when they reported in a French newspaper that the Ark was not on Mount Ararat, but Mount Judi further south. The measurements they reported were equivalent to the size of a football pitch. They found the bones of sea-animals, and the supposed grave of Noah nearby. This sighting which has never been confirmed by any other explorers, may have been in the imaginations of the journalists. In 1956, an explorer called Fernand Navarra, published a book in France describing how he had excavated planks and an L-shaped beam from a frozen lake on Mount Ararat. More planks found were later dated between BC 3000 and AD 700.

Recently, the Turkish authorities have closed off the area completely, so no new expeditions have been made in search of the Ark.

The spheres of Costa Rica

In the 1930s, when a forest was being cleared in Costa Rica, several granite spheres of all sizes were found. They were hand-made and perfectly smooth, and their diameters ranged from a few centimetres to 2 metres. The spheres are at least four centuries old, but that is about the only fact known about them. Who made them and why is a complete mystery.

A large crater on Mount Ararat is supposed to mark the site where Noah's Ark was stranded after the flood (see main text).

Mysterious stone spheres were found in a Costa Rican forest in the 1930s (see main text).

Two Dogon warriors (see main text). Part of the tribe who claim to have known for thousands of years about an invisible star only discovered in 1862.

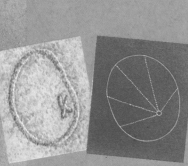

On the left is the Dogon sketch of Sirius B. Its egg-shaped orbit is accurate, although this may be a *coincidence* as they use the same shape around drawings of other things. The cross accurately marks the position of Sirius A. On the right is an astronomer's drawing of Sirius A and B.

BACK TO THE FUTURE

Every so often, *archaeologists* or other experts find evidence that certain groups of people seem to have possessed knowledge thousands of years before its modern scientific discovery. Often, this knowledge is about the stars or planets, but it can be about anything ranging from electric batteries to the precise layout of supposedly undiscovered countries.

People who believe that *aliens* landed many years ago and passed on advance information about the universe to our ancestors, think that all the cases of seemingly amazing knowledge are proof of their theories. In some cases, however, it has been shown that this gives no credit to the ingenuity and intelligence of our ancestors. Some experts think it more likely that early civilizations knew a great deal more than we think they did. Great engineering feats such as the Pyramids in Egypt and the *standing stone* circles worldwide, show what could be achieved without modern equipment and technology.

The Dogon people

The Dogon people of Mali, West Africa, live in an isolated place between the towns of Timbuktu and Ouagoudougou. They live in a traditional way, with no modern technology and limited contact with the outside world. In the 1930s two French *anthropologists* M. Griaule and G. Dieterlen, discovered that the Dogon had extensive and accurate information about several stars and planets. Their religion, in fact, is centred around the star Sirius B, which is the companion of Sirius A, or 'Dog Star'. While Sirius A is the brightest star in the night-sky Sirius B is totally invisible to the naked eye and was not spotted until 1862 by telescope. Despite this, the Dogon claim to have known for thousands of years that Sirius B exists, and that it is white and extremely small and heavy. They also know that it has an elliptical (or oval-shaped) *orbit* around Sirius A and completes one turn every 50 years. The Dogon say that the whole universe originated from Sirius B, and all living souls come from there and go to a third Sirius star after death (no third star has yet been discovered). The Dogon call Sirius B 'Po Tolo', which is roughly translated as 'crabgrass star', as the crabgrass seed is the smallest one the Dogon have.

Admiral Piri, a 16th century Turkish pirate, drew maps of the world which seemed to show a knowledge of geography before its time. Antarctica was not discovered until 1818, for instance, and yet it appears on Piri's map. Some say that he

The Dogon claim to have gained their knowledge about Sirius B from an alien, Nommo, who came to earth thousands of years ago from the star. Nommo, who is regarded as a god by the Dogon, is half-man and half-dolphin. When he landed he apparently pulled his spaceship into a hollow which filled with water as he was more comfortable that way.

Information about Sirius B was published in 1928 and it is possible that the Dogon could have heard about it and incorporated it into their religion before the two Frenchmen questioned them about it. The Dogon are adamant, however, that they have had their knowledge for much longer. It is also regarded as so sacred by them that only a few of the tribe know it, and no one knows all of it. It has been divided between the high priests. This would seem to suggest a much more ancient tradition than *sceptics* think. But as it cannot now be proven either way, it remains a tantalizing mystery.

The Mahabharata

The Mahabharata is a long, Indian poem, written during the second century AD. In it there are many accounts of battles between the heroes which seem to contain references to weapons and equipment that were not invented until this century. The hero, Krishna, for instance, uses arrows which behave like anti-ballistic missiles. He also kills his enemy with what sounds like a 'smart bomb' which seeks out its target using sound waves. Some of the equipment is so futuristic that it still has not been invented. One character, for instance, flies around in a vehicle which resembles space-ships in modern science fiction.

The most frightening part of the poem seems to accurately describe the effects of a nuclear explosion. It tells how the hero, Gurkha, threw one missile against three cities from his flying machine. It contained 'all the power of the universe' and rose up in a single column after exploding, destroying every living thing in the cities. The poem further describes what sound like the effects of nuclear radiation. Hair and nails fell out, food was contaminated and people threw themselves into water to try and wash off the poison. The accuracy of this description makes people believe the poet had a *vision* of the terrible weapons we possess today.

based the maps on those drawn by alien visitors thousands of years before. As there are inaccuracies in the maps, this seems unlikely but there is no explanation as to how Piri came by his information.

In the 1930s, a German archaeologist, Wilhelm Koenig, found clay pots in Iraq, which were 2000 years old. Each pot contained copper and iron rods, was sealed with bitumen, and showed traces of acid. Koenig realised that they were primitive electric batteries and they worked when he tested them. Since the first battery was thought to have been made in 1800, the find is baffling.

The ancient Sumerians, a race of people who lived about BC 3000, had an astonishing knowledge of the stars and planets. Our modern calendar is based on theirs, although they had no equipment with which to study the sky. In their calculations, they allowed for the fact that the earth wobbles on its axis as it turns, and they were also able to measure the distance between stars. They also recognized ten planets in the solar system but as yet we only acknowledge the existence of nine.

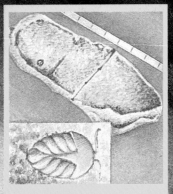

In 1968, William Meister, an amateur fossil collector, found a print of what appeared to be a human foot wearing a sandal, squashing a primitive trilobite (an early ancestor of shrimps) with the heel. The trilobite, thought to have become extinct 280 million years ago, would date the print as being 300-600 million years old, long before humans and most animals are thought to have existed, far less wearing sandals! The print was found in a rock in Utah, USA.

In 1932, gold prospectors in Wyoming, USA, came across the *mummified* remains of a middle-aged man only 35 centimetres tall. The find seemed to confirm local legends of a race of tiny people, but some scientists believe the mummy was that of a child with anencephaly; a disease which causes signs of ageing. As the mummy has since been lost, no further examinations are possible.

MYSTERIOUS RELICS

The theory that people did not begin to *evolve* from apes until 30 million years ago is well established. It is estimated that life has existed for about 600 million years so this makes us one of the youngest species on earth. Recently, some amazing finds have baffled scientists and made them doubt the accuracy of some theories and even the systems used to date ancient *fossils* and *relics*.

Fossilized footprints, claimed to be human, were found in Nevada, USA in 1882, in sandstone 225-280 million years old. This is 195-250 million years before man was believed to exist. Even more amazing are human footprints found beside those of a three-toed dinosaur although dinosaurs died out millions of years before man *evolved*. Some of these human prints are huge, suggesting that some of our ancestors were giants. In 1932, 13 fossilized prints were found that measured 55 × 25 centimetres, a similar size to the *apemen* prints found recently (see pages 24, 25). There are even claims that human skeletons measuring 2.90 metres have been found, and human skulls with horns and double rows of teeth. Remains of tiny humans have also been found. Minute flint tools were discovered in England in the late 19th century. The largest of these measured only 13 millimetres and many of them were half that length or shorter. Similar finds in other countries led some experts to think either that there were races of tiny people on earth, or the tools were made for decoration by skillful stone-age artists.

Some people believe that all these strange finds prove that the ancient *legends* of giants, fairies and little people are true. The finds certainly suggest that there is much we do not know about our past and our ancestors.

Out of place objects

It is not only remains of living things that are found out of their time and sometimes in very odd places, but objects too. One of the strangest of these discoveries was made between 1786 and 1788 in a quarry in Aix-en-Provence, France. About 15 metres down in the ground, workers found tools, coins and half-worked stones and the remains of a complete stonemason's yard which used almost identical tools to those of the 18th century finders although they must have been about 300 million years old.

One of the most amazing discoveries ever made was in 1856, by workmen building the railway tunnel between the Saint-Dizier and Nancy lines in France. A boulder of ancient limestone had just been broken open, and out of the stone fell a pterodactyl. The winged reptile,

The tools, originally wooden, had turned to stone, or *petrified*, during the time they had been in the ground. No one to this day can offer an explanation as to how the tools got there. If they are genuine, it implies that we have got our history all wrong, and people not only existed, but were very sophisticated long before the experts think was possible.

Living fossils

Strangely enough, there are hundreds of reports from people who claim to have found living animals inside solid pieces of rock and stone. There is never any passage through which the animal could have got in, and it is often lying in a cavity which is a perfect mould of itself, as if the rock or coal formed around it; a process which takes millions of years and needs enormous heat and pressure.

Usually, the animals found are frogs and toads, but there have also been shellfish, snakes, newts and lizards. Often, the animal lives for several days or weeks after its release, and can function perfectly normally, despite its long captivity and the fact that it probably never used its legs before. Sometimes, however, the animals have abnormalities such as no mouths, or joined legs or feet. They may also have difficulty breathing fresh air, and often change colour when exposed to the light. What baffles scientists most is the seemingly impossible amount of time some of the creatures appear to have spent in their prison; thousands or even millions of years. The whole thing is so strange, that some people believe it is magic, or that the creatures have somehow been *teleported* back in time (see page 3).

The dating process

There are a number of methods used to date ancient objects and remains. The trouble is that experts studying fossils or rocks, for example, do not always agree with the dating methods or theories used by other experts. Until dating methods are proved right or wrong, finding explanations for some of these mysterious discoveries, apparently out of their time and place, seems to be impossible.

…hich was thought to have died …ut 100 million years ago, just …ad time to croak feebly and flap …s wings before it died. The …reature's legs were joined by a …membrane and it had sharp …alons and teeth. The wingspan …as 3.20 metres and its skin was …ily and black.

At the beginning of this century, Mr W Clarke of Rugby, England, saw something move as he broke open a piece of coal in his fire. Grabbing it, he was astonished to find that it was a live toad. The animal had no mouth and was almost transparent, but survived for five weeks after its release from the coal.

When Toulon harbour in France was built, it was a well-known fact that the stones used for the paving often contained shellfish which were very much alive and apparently very tasty. Hard stones quarried at Ancona on the Adriatic were also said to contain a variety of shellfish which were also alive and edible.

MYSTERIOUS FOOTPRINTS

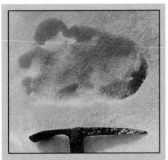

In 1951, the Everest explorer Eric Shipton saw a number of strange footprints which he could not identify. He took a photograph of one with an ice axe beside it to show the scale. The footprint measured 45 × 33 centimetres and had three small toes and one big toe. Many people who have seen the photograph, believe that it shows a Yeti's footprint.

In October, 1967, Roger Patterson and Bob Gimlin saw a female Bigfoot in Bluff Creek, Northern California. Patterson managed to shoot a ciné film of the creature in which she can be seen turning to look at him as she walks away. Analysis of her footprints confirmed the two men in their estimate of her height at about 2.15 metres. Although many scientists are unwilling to accept the film as genuine, there are also many who do.

For hundreds of years, experts have been baffled by reports of sightings of large man-like animals, or *'apemen'*, which have been seen as far apart as the West coast of America, to the Himalayas in Tibet. In America and Canada they are called Sasquatch, or 'Bigfoot', because of the huge size of footprints found. In Tibet they are Yetis, or 'Abominable Snowmen'. Similar animals have also been sighted in parts of Russia and Asia, where they are called Almas.

Most of the descriptions of these animals are very similar. They are usually between 2.50 and 3 metres tall, covered in long, reddish-brown hair, and with round, pointed heads. They are said to feed on berries and leaves but one witness saw a group of Bigfeet eating small rodents which they had dug out of hibernation. Occasionally, they have been said to attack people, although only when afraid or hungry – usually they are shy.

The six-day ordeal

In 1924, Albert Ostman, a construction worker, went on a gold-digging trip in British Columbia, Canada and set up camp opposite Vancouver Island. One night, he was woken by something picking him up in his sleeping bag. Several hours, and 40 kilometres later he was put down on the ground, and when he crawled out of his sleeping bag, saw that he was in the midst of a family of four Sasquatch. The father was 2.40 metres tall, the mother about 30 centimetres less. There were also two teenage children, a girl and a boy. For six days, Ostman was held captive by the Sasquatch and treated well by them although they refused to let him out of their sight. Ostman believed that they intended him to become the girl's 'husband', which would account for their behaviour. Eventually, he fired a shot from his rifle which confused and frightened his captors long enough for him to run away. His amazing story remained unkown until 1957. Ostman was so sure that no one would believe it, he kept quiet for 33 years.

Identifying apemen

If apemen do exist, they do not belong to any known species of animal. The tracks that have been found, although they sometimes resemble animals such as mountain gorillas or grizzly bears, certainly do not belong to either animal. Some

An American Indian man, Muchalat Harry, claimed to have been captured by a Bigfoot near Vancouver Island, Canada in 1928. Dressed only in underwear and in his sleeping bag, Harry was picked up and carried several kilometres to a Bigfoot settlement. In the morning he found himself surrounded by about twenty of

experts who are prepared to believe in apemen think that they may be a surviving species of primitive man, called *Neanderthal man*; a very early ancestor of present-day man, who was believed to have died out hundreds of thousands of years ago.

The Vietnam iceman

As apemen usually live in deep, often unexplored forests, many people have tried and failed to capture one, and most hunting trips end without even a glimpse or an apeman or his tracks. In 1969, however, a giant apeman preserved in a block of ice was seen by dozens of people in a travelling show in the USA. It was claimed that the 'iceman' was found in the Vietnam jungle after being shot in the head by a woman who was attacked by it. Two scientists examined the corpse and pronounced that it was a genuine Neanderthal man. Many people, however, remain convinced that the apeman was a clever rubber model as the body has now completely disappeared.

In 1884, a Bigfoot was supposedly captured in British Columbia. The creature, 1.38 metres tall, was named Jacko, but no tests were ever done to find out what he was. Nobody knows what happened to Jacko, although there were rumours that he was exhibited in a circus. If Jacko was a Bigfoot, he was a small specimen which suggests either that he was young, or that all sightings have been exaggerated. It is a frustrating example of evidence that has slipped through scientists' fingers, allowing the existence of apemen to remain an unproven mystery.

Evidence of apemen

Most of the evidence for Bigfeet, Yetis or Almas, is in the form of photographs and casts of footprints. In some cases this evidence is strong. In 1969, in Washington, USA, for instance, a trail of Bigfoot prints were found. There were 1089 prints in all, and from the shape of them it seemed that the creature had a crippled right foot. Some Tibetan monasteries claimed to possess ancient scalps of Yetis but when one was examined it was found to come from a goat-like animal called a southern serow.

The only real 'evidence' for the apeman is the eye-witness accounts and there are so many unexplored land-areas in the world, it is quite possible that many reports are true.

...e creatures who prodded at ...m and, thinking his underwear ...as skin, were alarmed at how ...ose and easily-torn it was. ...arry stayed very still and ...ventually, when the creatures ...st interest, he took the chance ...o escape. He was so shaken by ...e event, that his hair turned ...hite and he never left his village ...gain.

In 1941, during the Second World War, a Russian officer whose unit had been fighting in the Caucasus, examined a strange prisoner. He looked like an ape, was naked and dirty and had a vacant expression. The officer later heard that he had been executed as an army deserter. It is believed by many that he was an Alma (the Russian equivalent of a Yeti).

A female Alma called Zana is also said to have been in captivity in Russia for many years. At first violent, she eventually became domesticated and enjoyed drinking wine. She was said to have died in 1890, after giving birth to several children, the last of whom died in 1954.

WATER MONSTERS

Two-thirds of the world's surface is under water, most of which has never been explored, so it is quite believable that some huge, unidentifed creatures live in the world's seas and lakes. Thousands of people over many hundreds of years have reported seeing such monsters, and even today, there are at least two sightings of huge sea-serpents every year.

There are even more sightings of monsters in lakes, some of which are hardly big enough to provide food and shelter for such animals. Because of this, many scoff at reports of monsters and say they are a figment of the imagination. In some cases, however, reports are so consistent, that research is done to try to find and identify particular monsters (see pages 28, 29).

Close encounter with a sea-serpent

In 1966, two British army paratroopers, John Ridgway and Chay Blyth, rowed across the Atlantic Ocean in 92 days in a boat 6 metres long. One morning just before it was light, Ridgway saw a huge squirming creature in the water, right beside the boat. As it came straight towards him, he saw it clearly and judged that it was about twice as long as the boat, before it plunged away beneath them. After several seconds, there was an enormous splash behind the boat, and the creature was gone. Ridgway said later that it was like no animal he had ever seen before, and he could only suggest that it was a sea-serpent, although he had not believed in them before his trip.

Lake and river monsters

There are many famous lake and river monsters all over the world. In British Columbia, Canada, Lake Okanagan is said to be the home of a 9-metre long, snake-headed, blunt-nosed creature, nicknamed Ogopogo. Since 1700, at least 200 people have claimed sightings of Ogopogo, and many of the descriptions are similar. In 1968, five young waterskiers got so close to Ogopogo in their boat that they could see the brightly coloured scales on its back.

In Central Africa, there are strong *legends* amongst the local people about a monster described as half-elephant, half-dragon, which is supposed to live in the swamps of the Ubangi-

Lake Champlain, which stretches for 160 kilometres from Canada to Vermont and New York State, USA is said to be home to a monster known as 'Champ'. He has been seen on many occasions, and according to reports, has a snake-like head, three humps and shiny black skin, which is similar to descriptions of Scottish 'Nessie' (see page 28). In 1980, the town of Port Henry on Lake Champlain officially forbad the harrassment or injury of Champ.

In 1861 the crew of a French ship travelling from Spain to Tenerife, saw an enormous creature in the sea, whose size and nearness made the ship roll fiercely. Some of the crew harpooned the monster, but as they were hauling it aboard, it broke free, leaving behind a massive chunk of its tail. The creature, which could have been a giant squid, had a red, jelly-like body about 5 metres long, and eight long arms.

During August, 1817, many people reported seeing a 12-metre sea-serpent in Gloucester Harbour, Massachusetts, USA. The creature was dark-skinned, except for a white throat and stomach, and its body was as wide as a barrel all the way down to its tail. It moved about 50 kilometres an hour.

Congo basin. In 1980 and 1981, an American biologist, Dr Roy Mackal, led two expeditions to the region in search of the monster, known locally as mokele-mbembe. On the second trip, Dr Mackal found large footprints, the size of an elephant's, leading into a river. All the vegetation around them had been flattened in a way that suggested the creature moved like a reptile. Although Dr Mackal never saw it, he came away convinced of mokele-mbembe's existence.

Identifying water monsters

Those who do believe in water monsters think that they must either be completely undiscovered species, or that they are living members of species which were thought to have died out millions of years ago. The fact that most of the creatures, if they exist, live in the deepest, darkest waters, makes it possible that they could have survived in small numbers without us knowing about them. The sea-serpent seen by John Ridgway, for instance, may be a kind of toothed whale called a zeuglodon, an animal thought to be *extinct*. Exciting evidence that some 'extinct' species are actually alive, was provided in 1938, when a coelacanth – a fish thought to have died out 70 million years ago – was caught off the coast of South Africa. Another 1.50-metre long specimen, caught in 1979, convinced those who were still *sceptical*.

Some of the lake monsters may turn out to be known species that have been stranded in the wrong place. Experts believe, for instance, that the White River monster in Arkansas, USA, is probably an elephant seal which frightens people because no one expects to see one there. There are also some reports which are doubted because they are of sightings in lakes which are too small to support a large creature. Lough Nahooin in West Ireland, for example is hardly more than a pond and yet it is supposed to support at least one resident 3.60-metre monster.

One thing that all the monsters have in common is that they refuse to be finally caught and identified, and they are very camera-shy. Until they are all finally proven to be something quite ordinary, however, the sheer number of sightings must leave room for doubt.

In 1980, it was reported in a Chinese newspaper that a creature which looked like a dinosaur had been seen in Wenbu Lake in Tibet. Apparently, it ate a yak which had been allowed to graze by the lake on its way to market.

In 1977, a Japanese trawler netted the rotting remains of an animal thought to be (like Scotland's Nessie) a *plesiosaur* – a creature supposed to have died out 70 million years ago. This, however, is only a calculated guess as the body smelt so bad that the crew had to throw it back in the sea. Tissue samples which were saved were too decomposed to be identified beyond all doubt. The body weighed 1800 kilograms, and was 9.60 metres long. It was caught at a depth of 270 metres.

27

THE LOCH NESS MONSTER

Loch Ness, near Inverness in the North of Scotland, is the deepest, darkest loch in Britain. The bottom of the loch shelves steeply under the water and the channel that runs up the middle averages more than 200 metres deep. In places it is thought that the loch is as deep as 290 metres. Peat particles suspended in the water make it very difficult to take underwater pictures of anything in the loch, as even a powerful underwater light will only penetrate a few centimetres in the deeper parts.

For years, there have been hundreds of sightings reported of a huge, unidentified animal in, and sometimes beside, the loch. Some people have even managed to take photographs although 'Nessie' (as the monster is called) does seem to be very camera-shy. Scientists have also been trying to overcome the difficult conditions and find conclusive proof that the monster (or colony of monsters) does or does not exist. No one, however, has ever found anything such as teeth or remains, that could have come from the monster. Until something substantial is found, most scientists will not be convinced that she exists.

Early sightings of Nessie

The very first recorded sighting of the monster was in AD 565 when the writer Adamnan wrote of how a monster in that area had killed a swimmer and had been commanded to leave by St Columba. After that, there was silence until 1930, when a piece appeared in a local newspaper about three men who saw Nessie from a small boat while they were fishing. This prompted people to write in with similar stories, and soon the national newspapers took up the story and Nessie became famous. From the sightings and photographs, a picture of Nessie can be built up. She seems to have a long neck, dark grey/brown skin, a large head and white throat, a bulky body with four small 'paddles' or flippers, and three humps down her back. Estimates of her overall length have varied from about 6-8 metres. Scientists who do believe that the monster exists, think that there must be more than one and that they do vary in size.

In 1934, Nessie was seen lurching across the loch-side road by a startled medical student called Arthur Grant as he was riding home on his motor-bike one moonlit night. He said that the creature was about 6 metres long, had a long neck and 4 flipper-like legs. Grant thought that the animal looked like a cross between a plesiosaur and a member of the seal family. He chased it into the undergrowth but the animal disappeared into the loch.

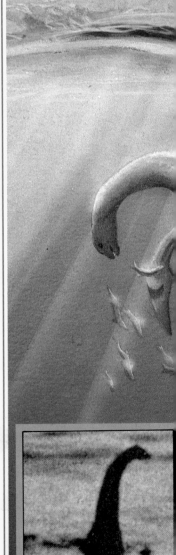

One of the earliest photographs of the Loch Ness monster was taken in 1934 by R K Wilson, a London surgeon. It is claimed to show the head and long neck of the monster.

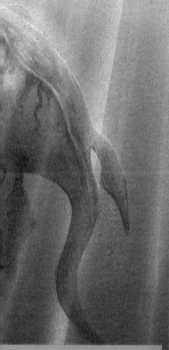

This picture of Nessie is based on photographic evidence obtained in 1975 during an investigation into the monster, led by the American scientist Dr Robert Rines.

Evidence of Nessie

In 1962, the Loch Ness Investigation Bureau was formed to try to find evidence of Nessie. They searched the loch using the most modern cameras, lights and *sonar* equipment (which works by bouncing sound waves from objects moving in the water which are then traced out as images on paper). Due to lack of funds, however, the Bureau had to shut down in 1972, without having found their proof. The American Academy of Applied Science took over the research and made several expeditions in search of Nessie. In 1972, using a combination of sonar beam and camera, they managed to get an exciting photograph of what looks like a flipper. Evidence also showed that there were two 'objects' in the water. In 1975, the same team went on a similar expedition with modernized equipment. This time they picked up many signals from the sonar beam scanner, but the 'object' had kicked up so much silt from the bottom that most of the photographs were blank. One, however, seemed to show a pinkish body with a long neck and two short horns on its head.

Since 1975, no spectacular evidence has been found, but there have been some advances in the research. It has been shown, for instance, that the loch could support several large animals and that there is plenty of food and oxygen. New sonar equipment has also shown many interesting unidentified objects, one of which moved and dived in the way that an animal the size of Nessie would. A large expedition mounted in 1987, also showed some tantalizing sonar findings, but did not manage to take any photographs.

What is Nessie?

If Nessie is not a figment of the imagination she is certainly a very strange creature indeed. There are many theories about what she could be, ranging from a leftover dinosaur to a spirit conjured up by an evil magician. Some think that she may be a giant slug, or snail, or an overgrown seal. The most popular theory, however, is that she is a large water reptile called a *plesiosaur* thought to have been *extinct* for 70 million years. Some are even more specific and say that she is an elasmosaur, which is a kind of plesiosaur.

Whatever Nessie is, she seems determined to live in peace and keep her secret for some time to come.

The most recent photograph of Nessie, taken in 1977 by Anthony Shiels, is similar to the 1934 view of the monster.

In October, 1987, twenty boats all carrying sonar equipment, sailed abreast up the central channel of Loch Ness for three days and made a 'curtain sweep' of the water. Three large, moving objects were contacted at a depth of 180 metres. These results are still being analysed in America, although the objects all appear to be the size of an average shark.

This photograph showing Nessie's three humps was taken by Lachlan Stuart in 1951.

In 1935, the researcher Harry Price set up an experiment with the Indian firewalker Kuda Bux, in a garden in Surrey, England. The pit dug for the fire was 3.50 metres long, and the temperature of the coals was 1400°C – hotter than the melting point of steel. Bux walked over the fire twice, with no injury. Two witnesses who tried it themselves, received bad burns. It was established that no cheating was involved, but no conclusions about firewalking were reached.

In 1672, the Englishman John Evelyn recorded in his diary the feats of an extraordinary fire-handler called Richardson. He apparently ate a molten beer glass, drank a flaming concoction of pitch, wax and sulphur, held a red-hot iron between his teeth, and, most spectacularly of all, cooked a raw oyster on top of a live coal which he had balanced on his tongue.

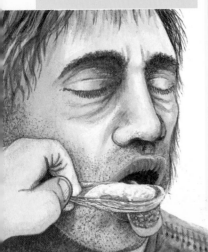

FIREPROOF PEOPLE

It is a fact that in many countries all over the world, there are people who regularly walk through fires which are hot enough to cripple or kill them, without even a blister to show for it. Usually, firewalking forms a part of a religious ceremony, and those who practise it often prepare for days beforehand, fasting and praying. Some say that this preparation is necessary so that the mind and body are totally controlled. There are those, however, who perform firewalking for tourists, almost like a circus act. They do not prepare themselves in any way, and they are never injured although tourists who join in the firewalk sometimes receive terrible burns.

Firewalking in Sri Lanka

In Kataragama, a remote area in South East Sri Lanka, a religious firewalking festival every August is preceded by a day of bearing terrible wounds and burdens to prove faith. Some people are whipped and some have skewers put through their cheeks. Others cut themselves with knives or are suspended for hours from dozens of metal hooks attached to the body. The amazing thing is that no one seems to feel any pain, and blood does not flow from the wounds.

At the end of the day, the people are in a state of religious *frenzy*, and it is then that many do the firewalk. The pit in which the fire has been prepared is 6-9 metres long, and the temperature is between 800°C and 1000°C. After a ritual wash, the candidates for the walk (usually 50 or more) go into the fire pit, repeating a Hindu prayer. They emerge exhausted but unhurt, and the day's activities are over for another year.

Fire-handlers

The ability to touch and handle fire without injury is an ancient tradition all over the world. Thousands of years ago blacksmiths were held in high esteem as the original 'masters of fire' and many of them were reputedly able to handle red-hot metals, swallow burning coals and walk over embers in bare feet. Now, fire-handling is more of a curiosity than an essential part of religious life, and those who possess 'the gift' are often rather frowned upon as showpeople.

In 1871, Nathan Coker, an American blacksmith, proved in front of the whole town that

Firewalking is often performed as part of a religious ceremony Many Indian fakirs ('holy men') work themselves into a religiou frenzy before the walk, which they claim is an important par of the fireproofing process. Before dancing in the flames they demonstrate their fire immunity by handling the fire with bare hands. Amazingly neither they nor their clothes a damaged during the ritual.

he could withstand fire. He kept a white-hot shovel on the soles of his bare feet until it cooled down, swilled molten lead shot around his mouth until it solidified, then picked out glowing coals from his forge with bare hands. Coker claimed that he had always had the gift of *fire immunity*, and did not take it to be anything particularly special.

The famous *medium* Daniel Dunglas Home often demonstrated his fire-handling ability during *seances*. More than once, he would rub his face in a coal fire while in a trance, or pick out glowing coals with his bare hands. One remarkable aspect of Home's ability, which is shared by many tribal fire-handlers, is that he could pass on his fire immunity to others. During one seance, he put a burning coal on the head of his host, pulling the hair up round it in a pyramid. He would also hand coals to people who would touch them without injury.

Theories and experiments

It has been proved that there are no cheap tricks in fire immunity. The fires are really hot, and firewalkers do not treat their feet with any barrier ointment. What is not clear is how it is done. Some physics experts say that it is a matter of gymnastics; that it is possible to walk over extremely hot coals if it is done quickly and evenly, as no part of the foot would be in contact with the coals for long. This theory, however, does not explain why some firewalkers seem able to stroll as slowly as they like over the coals, or why some people who attempt the firewalk at the same pace as other participants get burnt.

The answer seems to be that handling fire and walking over coals is the combined result of *mind over matter*, the belief that it can be done, and enormous courage. Where firewalking is part of the culture, some people are taught gradually how to do it and how to develop the right mental attitude. Others, carried away by the exciting atmosphere of a firewalking display, can suddenly find themselves taking part in the ritual safely and confidently.

In 1981, interesting experiments were done on an Indian *fakir* who claimed to be immune to pain of all kinds. When he and a group of volunteers were given electric shocks while their brain waves were recorded, it was found that the fakir could slow down his brain waves as if he were asleep during the shocks.

In 1731, Marie Souet, a follower of the executed French heretic François de Paris, exhibited her fire immunity in front of many witnesses. Wrapped in a linen sheet, Marie went into a rigid *trance* and was suspended over a blazing fire for 35 minutes. The flames licked the sheet, but neither Marie nor the sheet were even scorched.

In 1922, the Maharajah of Mysore, India, invited a French bishop to witness a firewalking ceremony led by a Muslim *mystic*. First, a palace servant was pushed into the flames, and after a terrified struggle, a smile broke over his face and he emerged unscathed. Next, the Maharajah's entire band walked into the fire, with the flames licking around their instruments and sheets of music. They too emerged unhurt. The mystic claimed to have taken the burning of the fire on himself, which is why no one was injured. He then collapsed in agony, asking for water.

's photograph, taken after a walking ceremony, shows no n of blistering on the fakir's t.

ODD BODIES

Some people seem to have bodies which, without any effort, can do such things as *levitate* (float in the air,) become longer or shorter, or even give people electric shocks when touched. Scientists are baffled by these strange abilities which seem to defy all natural laws, and many assume that trickery is involved. The cases, however, are so numerous and well-documented that this is hard to believe.

In the past, it was thought that such things as levitation were either signs of devil *possession* or extreme holiness. Some people were made saints after reports of them 'taking off' while at prayer. It was believed that these things could only happen with the help of God, angels or other spirits. Some now think, however, that the human mind can sometimes overcome natural barriers such as gravity and either deliberately or unconsciously do things which would normally be impossible.

Levitation

Many *mediums* regularly used to levitate not only themselves, but objects and sometimes other people. During many *seances*, tables would lift off the ground or people would rise off the floor in their chairs. One of the most famous and successful 'levitators' was Daniel Dunglas Home, who regularly took off while in a *trance*. On one occasion he is said to have floated out of one window and in at another.

Levitation is often practised by holy people and *mystics*. The French explorer Alexandra David-Neel, who spent 14 years in Tibet, described one holy man whose training had made him so light, he had to walk around in iron chains to prevent himself floating off.

Body lengthening

Some people's bodies can grow several centimetres in a matter of seconds. This is called elongation and usually happens while a person is in a trance, a state of religious *ecstasy* or in cases of convulsions caused by medical conditions such as *hysteria*. In *yoga*, bodily elongation is one of the eight 'siddhus', or magic powers, gained through *meditation*.

A man called Angelo Faticoni, from Florida, USA, who died in 1931, was widely known as the 'human cork'. For some reason he had the strange ability to float in water no matter how much he was weighted down. Faticoni was so buoyant, he could sleep curled up in the water and swim with lead weights tied to his ankles. He once swam across the Hudson River with a chair weighted with lead tied to his foot.

After a long illness in 1877, in which she suffered fits and *hallucinations*, Caroline Clare of Ontario, Canada, found that she had developed the alarming ability to discharge electricity and attract metal like a magnet. Cutlery would stick fast to her body and someone else had to pull it off.

In 1936, a tea planter living in Southern India witnessed a convincing levitation by the Indian performer Subbayah Pullavar who had been practising yoga for 20 years. First, he sprinkled water round a small tent, then stepped inside it. Minutes later, the tent was taken away and Pullavar was floating with one hand resting on a stick. Photographs were taken and the witnesses passed their hands under his body to make sure he was not attached to anything. Later, Pullavar's limbs were so stiff, they had to be massaged gently back to normal.

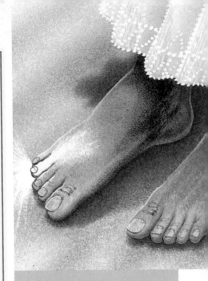

One respected mystic from Dacca, India, called Anandamayi Ma (also known as 'Mother') could expand, shrink, or bounce up and down like a rubber ball while in a trance.

In 1878, a Canadian girl called Esther Cox, who was the victim of a *poltergeist* (or 'noisy ghost') attack, was pulled out of bed one night by a strange force. On the middle of the floor, she began to inflate all over, then, after four loud bangs, her body returned to normal.

Electric people

Although each cell of the body can generate a small amount of electricity, it should not be possible for people to become so highly charged that they can give electric shocks, or make objects spring away from them. In the 1890s, however, a young girl called Jennie Morgan from Missouri, USA, was so charged that sparks flew from her body, animals avoided her and people who touched her were sometimes knocked unconscious by the shock.

People have also become magnets. In 1890, a young boy called Louis Hamburger showed he could dangle a 2-kilogram jar of iron filings from the tips of three fingers.

Glowing people

Many people seem to have been able to generate light from various parts of the body. Oddly enough, this often happens to those who are either ill, or actually dead, although there are also accounts of religious people who have become sources of 'divine' light. Saint Ludwina, whose biography was written in 1911, was apparently flooded with light every night in her cell, some of which seemed to come from her own body.

Some experts think that glowing may be linked to the germs, or bacteria, that cause some diseases, or may be a combination of skin chemicals forming a *luminous* substance.

Kirlian photographs

The Russian scientists Semyon and Valentina Kirlian demonstrated that every living thing has a glowing 'aura' which is normally invisible to the naked eye but can be photographed. It was also shown that if a portion was cut off a leaf, the 'aura' still showed the cut-off portion as if it were still there. It is not known if the auras are electric, magnetic, or something more mysterious altogether.

In 1869, a strange case of a glowing toe was reported. Apparently, an American woman found that each night when she went to bed, the fourth toe on her right foot was glowing. When she rubbed it, the glowing would spread up her foot. No amount of washing could dim the light, which usually lasted for about ¾ hour. Nasty smelling fumes were also said to be given off from the toe.

The Kirlians (see main text) demonstrated that every living thing has a glow, or an 'aura' around it that is normally invisible. Some *psychics* claim to be able to see coloured auras around people.

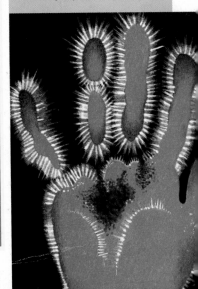

STRANGE VISIONS AND IMAGES

The idea of seeing whole armies marching through the sky, or cities floating hundreds of metres above the ground, or faces that appear for no reason on walls, is ridiculous to many people. Yet there are hundreds of reports of such strange sightings, many of which have been seen, and sometimes even photographed, by witnesses.

In 1890, the people of Ashland, Ohio, were amazed when a *vision* of a large city appeared right over the town at four o'clock in the afternoon. Some thought it was a revelation from heaven, although most seemed to think it bore a resemblance to either of the nearby towns of Mansfield and Sandusky. The vision was never repeated and remains a mystery to this day.

The angels of Mons

One of the most famous series of visions which were shared by many soldiers in 1914, happened at the Battle of Mons in Belgium during the First World War. The British army were in retreat from the Germans, and were heavily outnumbered. According to many, various apparitions were seen in the sky during the retreat. Some saw angels and saints, and others saw phantom soldiers with bows, aiming at the advancing Germans. One night, a Lieutenant-Colonel and all his brigade saw an army of ghostly cavalrymen riding alongside them.

A writer called Arthur Machen, who published a short story in a London newspaper about Saint George and a spectral army intervening on behalf of the British at Mons, claimed that reports of the visions were inspired by his story. Angry soldiers, however, wrote in to deny this, saying that many witnesses testified to seeing the visions.

Spontaneous images

When Dean Vaughan of Llandaff, Wales died in 1902, people were astonished when a likeness of his face suddenly appeared in a damp patch on the wall of Llandaff Cathedral. Some said that the likeness was a *coincidence*, but many remained convinced that it was a 'message' from Dean Vaughan himself.

Sometimes, images have appeared on objects which seem to mark some event that has just happened. In 1680, for instance, when a *comet* appeared over Rome, Italy, many were astounded when a hen laid an egg with a good reproduction

In 1876, the American General George Custer and his cavalry regiment of 600 men set off to fight the Sioux Indians in Montana. As the regiment left it appeared to many of those seeing them off that half of them rode into the sky and vanished completely. A month later, General Custer and half his regiment were cornered and killed by Sioux warriors. Many thought the vision of the disappearing army was an *omen* of the massacre.

In 1887, a man called Willoughby claimed to photograph a vision of the ci[ty] Bristol, England, which appeared in the skies of Alas[ka] (The spire of Mary Redcliffe church is clearly visible.) This sighting is only one of many

were reported in following years. Traditionally, the city is visible in Alaska every year between 21st June and 10th July. Alaskan Indians claim that it has appeared for hundreds of years, long before white settlers came to the area.

of the comet surrounded by stars on the shell. The image was not on the surface of the shell, but seemed to be part of it, thus seeming to rule out any human tampering.

Spontaneous images are even harder to explain than sky visions. They are substantial, can be touched and photographed and they often last for years.

Controlled images

Some people claim to be able to produce images by thinking about them hard enough. Although it is usually people with *psychic* powers who do this, many researchers think that the ability may be more widespread. It has been noticed, for instance, that people sometimes seem to cause odd images, or over-exposures to appear on ordinary camera-film for no apparent reason.

In the 1890s, the famous *medium* Eusapia Palladino could produce images of her own face impressed into putty in sealed containers. She had no access to the putty and investigators found no evidence of cheating. It seemed she really produced the outlines through a concentrated burst of will-power.

Theories

Many visions and images are religious and, in the past, they were usually associated with exceptionally saintly people and taken as a sign from God. In the Bible's New Testament, for instance, John has a spectacular vision of the end of the world and the city of New Jerusalem. Some researchers think that such visions are *hallucinations*, caused by over-zealous spiritual fervour.

In cases where many witnesses see the same vision, it is thought by some that it is an hallucination on a grander scale, and that people in a crowd can be influenced by each other into a state of *mass hysteria* where they all believe they see the same thing.

For many, 'rational' explanations cannot account for all the evidence of visions and spontaneous images. Some think that thoughts may be capable of being made solid and transferred from the mind onto solid objects. This is called *thought projection*. Some researchers believe that thought projection accounts for other strange things such as *UFOs*, ghosts, and even lake monsters. Others think that the sightings represent a genuine mystery that is yet to be understood.

In 1923, 25 years after the death of Dean Liddell of Oxford, England, a strikingly accurate image of his face appeared in a damp patch on the wall of Christ Church, Oxford. The face was still there when the wall was covered up during the building of a new altar in 1931. No one knows if it is still visible.

In 1935, Mrs Gertrude Smith of Pennsylvania, USA, found that she could will her hens to lay eggs with patterns on the shells. She would stand outside the hen-house and concentrate on the image she wanted on the eggs. Amongst her many successes were eggs with sunflower petals, her own initials, and even one with triangular sides. She eventually became frightened by her ability and stopped using it.

REMARKABLE HAPPENINGS

Sometimes extraordinary events happen which are never repeated and remain isolated mysteries in the history of the world. There are other rare events which, although they have happened more than once, continue to defy any explanation and baffle all those who investigate them.

The great Siberian explosion

On 30th June, 1908, in a remote area of unexplored Siberian forest called the Tunguska Basin, an explosion occurred and the shock waves went round the entire world twice. As much as 1300 kilometres from the blast, equipment registered a force equal to a major earthquake, and a Trans-Siberian train stopped because the driver thought it had been derailed. For several months there were spectacular sunsets and sunrises in the northern hemisphere, and in many places it was light enough to read a newspaper at midnight. There were also many reports of odd-shaped clouds.

To this day, no one knows what caused the massive explosion which could have killed millions of people if it had happened in a populated area. When a Russian scientist, Leonid Kulik, was appointed to investigate it in 1921, all he found were 10,000 square kilometres of flattened forest. He believed that a huge *meteorite* crashed, but no debris was found and eye-witnesses claimed to have seen a light change course before it hit the ground – something no heavenly body would do.

Some believe that the explosion was caused by a nuclear-powered *alien UFO* crashing onto earth. Although radiation levels read normal by the time they were checked 50 years later, some things do point towards a nuclear solution (although not necessarily to the UFO idea). Reindeer herds near the blast were blistered, and a pillar of fire was seen which sounds like the 'mushroom cloud' associated with nuclear explosions. Also, local species of plant and insects were changed. As there is no concrete evidence one way or another, it will probably always remain a mystery.

The Devil's hoofprints

One February morning, during the hard British winter of 1855, the people of Devon, England,

An enormous explosion flattened a huge expanse of the Siberian forest in 1908. No one can explain the cause of the blast, although theories range from a giant meteorite to a nuclear explosion (see main text).

This photograph shows some of the devastation after the explosion.

'e Devil's hoofprints' (see
n text) appeared overnight
oss Devon, England, in 1855.
h horseshoe-shaped print
10 centimetres long and the
ts were 20 centimetres
rt. No animal or bird is known
hove in the way the
terious creature did – it
h appeared to 'jump' over
walls and haystacks, and
ked over roofs with ease.

woke to see a continuous line of horseshoe-shaped hoofprints stretched over snow-covered countryside for 65 kilometres. The strange prints were carefully placed one after the other; something which would have been impossible for a four-legged animal and difficult even for a two-legged one. The oddest thing of all was that the prints went over rooftops as well as the ground. They also stopped dead in front of high walls and haystacks, only to begin again on the other side with never any sign that anything had climbed over the obstacles. This led some to believe that the creature was a bird, although no known bird made such prints or moved in the way the prints suggested. The most popular explanation, however, was that the Devil himself, who is supposed to have a hoof-shaped print, visited Devon that night.

The mystery of the hoofprints was never solved. Some said at the time that they were made by an escaping balloon from Devonport dockyard which trailed a hoof-shaped attachment over the countryside. Some thought this had been hushed up because of the damage to property it had caused which the authorities did not want to pay for. As there is no proof of this story, however, it cannot be counted as fact.

Spontaneous human combustion

Although some doctors are reluctant to accept the possibility, evidence points to the fact that some people literally go up in flames for no apparent reason. This has been called *spontaneous human combustion*. It used to be thought that it only happened to people who drank a lot of alcohol, which burns easily and could act as a sort of fuel. There are too many cases, however, in which it is known that the victim was neither a drinker nor a smoker for this to be a valid theory.

One of the best-documented cases of spontaneous human combustion happened in 1951 to Mrs Mary Reeser of Florida, USA. When she was found there was no sign of a general fire in her room but all that was left of Mrs Reeser was a piece of her liver, a shred of backbone and one foot still in a black satin slipper. A pile of newspapers a few centimetres away had not been touched, although the mirror had cracked, probably due to intense heat, and the door knob was too hot to touch. Although the case was investigated by more than one leading doctor, none could offer any explanation for the tragedy.

Occasionally it has been known for people to burst into flames for no reason. This is called spontaneous human combustion (see main text). Many writers in the 18th and 19th centuries refer to this *phenomenon* in their books, including Charles Dickens, the famous Victorian novelist. Doctors, however, are often reluctant to accept that it really happens.

PEOPLE WITH SECRETS

Occasionally, people become famous because they have a well-kept secret or leave behind them some great mystery which is never solved. Writers and historians may try for years to piece together the facts, often with no luck whatsoever. The mysterious people then become *legends* along with their strange stories.

The man in the iron mask

The 'man in the iron mask', died in the French Bastille prison in 1703. No one knew who he was or why he had been locked up and guarded so carefully. In 1847, the French writer, Alexander Dumas, made him famous by claiming in a book that the man was the French King Louis XIV's twin brother, locked up so that he would never try to claim the throne, and masked to keep people from noticing his resemblance to the king. There is, however, no evidence for this story.

What is known about the masked man is that he was a prisoner for 34 years, and there were strict instructions from the king that he was to be killed if he tried to talk to anyone about himself. He did wear a mask, but it was black velvet and not iron – a much less cruel way of concealing his identity.

It is also fairly certain that the man's name was Eustache Dauger. What is not known however, is why such care was taken to conceal his identity. One theory is that Eustache's father was also Louis XIV's real father, thus making the prisoner and the king half-brothers, and the king illegitimate. New evidence, however, seems to point away from this theory, leaving the mystery as unsolved as ever.

Kaspar Hauser – the wild boy

In 1828, a 17-year-old boy turned up in Nuremburg, Germany. He was dressed in rags, could hardly talk, and carried two letters addressed to an army captain. One seemed to be from an adopted father, asking the captain to take the boy into the army, and the other looked as if it was a note written years before by Kaspar's mother when she abandoned him. When the letters were examined, however, it was obvious they had been written by the same person and at the same time. Kaspar's clothes were badly fitted, as if they were not his own. The boy behaved as if he had never been with people before, and repeated the same words and phrases over and

A mysterious man called Fulcanelli published a book in 1926, claiming that gothic cathedrals (such as Notre Dame in Paris) contained the secrets of *alchemy*, the ultimate aim of which is to transform oneself into a 'superhuman' being who could live forever. Fulcanelli himself is claimed to have known the secret of eternal youth, and although he was 80 in 1924, he was apparently seen 30 years later looking young and fresh. Fulcanelli became a cult figure and was hailed as a master of magic and knower of great secrets.

The man in the iron mask (see main text) was kept locked up for 34 years in various French jails. His mask was really made of black velvet, not iron. No one knows why he was imprisoned, or why his identity was kept secret.

over again, as if he had been taught them like a parrot.

Kaspar soon became famous all over Germany. At first, he was very sensitive to any new taste or smell, and everyone noticed how acute his eyesight and hearing were, like an animal's. Gradually he learned to speak, and said that he had been kept in a tiny room for as long as he could remember, and given only bread and water. He never saw anyone, his food being left while he was asleep. Occasionally his water would taste bitter and he would fall into a deep sleep, waking up to find his hair and nails cut and his straw bedding changed. Eventually, Kaspar said, a man came who taught him a few phrases, gave him the two letters and took him to Nuremberg, leaving him at the city gates. Some who heard this story believed that Kaspar must be of royal blood, but was hidden away for some reason.

Kaspar was taken round all the courts of Europe. He became plump and vain, enjoying all the attention heaped on him. In 1833, however, when Kaspar was back in Germany, he was attacked and received a fatal stab-wound in his side. Some believed that he staged the whole attack himself to get attention, but stabbed himself too hard and died accidentally. Kaspar denied this before he died, and his death, like his life, seems destined to remain a mystery.

The amazing Comte de Saint-Germain

In 1756, a man was introduced at the French court who caused a sensation by claiming to be hundreds of years old. He looked about 50 and could talk knowledgeably about many subjects and about people who were long-dead as if he had known them. He attended many dinner parties but never ate a thing, saying that he lived off a special *elixir* prepared only by himself. Although Saint-Germain was popular, many disliked his boastful manner and thought he was a fake. Because of this, he moved around from country to country, at one point even being made a Russian general.

Saint-Germain is supposed to have died in 1784 but people have claimed that he is still alive today and there have been many reported 'sightings' of him over the years. In 1972, a man named Richard Chanfray appeared on French TV claiming to be the deathless Saint-Germain, and to have the ability to turn lead into gold, which he apparently demonstrated.

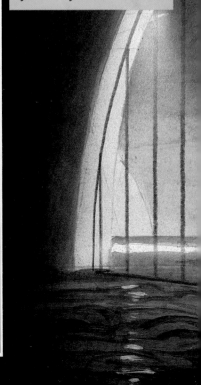

In 1901, a poor French priest called Béranger Saunière found some parchments in the church at Rennes-le-Château on which were coded messages. Not long after, Saunière became extremely rich, but refused to say how. It is thought that with the help of a secret organization called the Priory of Sion, the priest cracked the complex codes and found treasure which had been buried for hundreds of years. No one yet knows exactly what it was, although it is thought to be connected with some shattering secret guarded by the Priory of Sion.

Many people have reported a strange feeling of panic while climbing the Scottish mountain Ben MacDhui. Others claim to have seen a huge grey shadow which has been called 'the grey man of Ben MacDhui'. Strange singing has also been heard there. One young man who spent the night on the mountain saw a 6-metre tall creature, covered in brown hair, walking away from him. Footprints photographed on the mountain have also led some to think there may be a yeti (see page 24) living there.

According to the story of El Dorado (see main text), the ceremony to appoint a new chief involved throwing gold into the lake after he had covered his body with gold dust to make himself glint in the sun. Much of the treasure has been stolen from the lake, but some say these ceremonies still go on in secret.

MYSTERIOUS PLACES

Some places seem to have a kind of life of their own – a special atmosphere which may have been created by a great historical event taking place there, or may just be a 'feeling' which is there for no obvious reason. Such places become steeped in *legend* and the mystery grows as the stories are passed from generation to generation attracting researchers and the simply curious to investigate.

Atlantis

One of the greatest mysteries of all time is that surrounding the legendary lost continent of Atlantis, said to have disappeared under the Atlantic Ocean in a day and a night about 10,000 years ago. This supposedly great civilization was first written about by the Greek writer Plato, and ever since there has been fierce debate about whether or not Atlantis really existed.

In the original account, the Atlantians were highly skilled engineers and architects, and had a magnificent capital city surrounded by a complex system of canals. They were a mighty power, but went into a decline, and the people were punished by the gods for their immoral behaviour and destroyed.

Later additions to this story say that the people were magicians and *mediums* and brought about their own destruction through the use of black magic. Some even say that they destroyed themselves with the equivalent of a nuclear bomb.

Many people have tried to find concrete proof that Atlantis existed but there is no real evidence. Some people with *psychic* powers however, insist that such a place did exist. One *psychometrist* (someone who can tell the history of an object through touching it) gave a detailed account of Atlantis when handed a small stone statue of unknown origin.

El Dorado

For many years, treasure-hunters went in search of the legendary gold of El Dorado which was said to be somewhere in South America. The treasure was supposed to have gathered at the bottom of a certain lake as the result of a local tribal ceremony to appoint a new chief. According to the story, he would be taken out to the middle of the lake where he stripped, covered himself in gold dust, and made offerings of gold to the gods, throwing

Many people have searched for the lost continent of Atlantis, said to have sunk into the Atlantic Ocean without trace about 10,000 years ago. Some believe that survivors of the disaster founded such civilizations as ancient Egypt, and built the great pyramids. Others think that the continent may still be 'alive' under the water, and may even be the source of *UFOs* and odd disappearances such as those that happen in the Bermuda Triangle (see pages 4,5 & 16, 17).

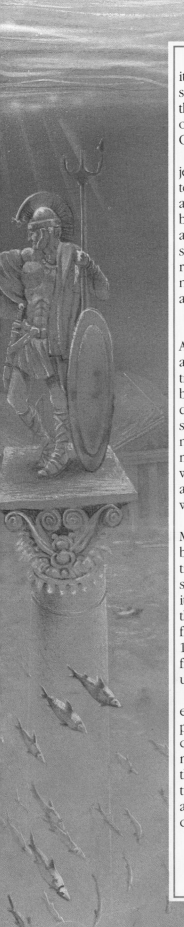

it deep into the waters. The spectators on the shore were also supposed to throw in treasures at this point. Many people tried to find this lake full of treasures, and eventually it was discovered in Colombia.

The earliest attempt to retrieve the gold and jewels was made in 1545, when slaves were made to form a human chain from the shore to the top of a nearby mountain, and drain the lake using buckets. The level fell 2.70 metres, and apparently a number of gold objects were taken from the shallower waters. Since then, more gold has been recovered, but the Colombian government has now passed laws to protect the site against adventurers.

The Money Pit

A very different kind of treasure-hunt was attempted by many people over 200 years on the tiny Oak Island, Newfoundland. In 1795, three boys found a pit which they were sure had been dug by pirates and was full of treasure. They made several attempts to dig into the pit, but there were no signs of reaching any treasure. About every 3 metres, they struck a platform made either of wood or flagstones. Eventually, they had to abandon the dig as the pit constantly filled with water when it was left.

It was many years before it was realized that the Money Pit was actually linked to the nearby beach by a flood tunnel, which filled the pit at every high tide. Whoever built the system was obviously a skilled engineer, and had devised a way of making it almost impossible for anyone to rob it before the tide flooded in. Many tried to block off the flood tunnel but with no success. It was not until 1897 that a second flood tunnel, deeper than the first, was found by one of the long line of unsuccessful treasure hunters.

A great deal of money and effort was put into excavating the Money Pit over the years. Five people even lost their lives in the course of all the dangerous digging and pumping. In 1967 a huge mechanical digger was used and although it sifted through everything and destroyed all trace of the tunnel in the process, no treasure was ever found and no one knows to this day who built such a complicated pit or for what reason.

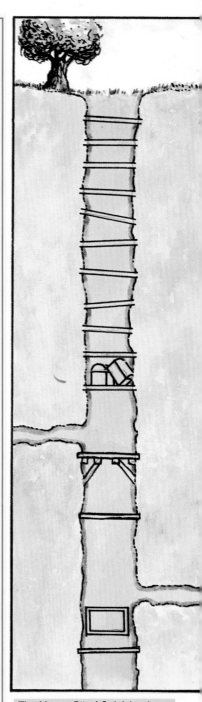

The Money Pit of Oak Island, Newfoundland (see main text), was discovered in 1795. The diagram above shows its elaborate structure with the protective flood tunnels built in at two levels. Until 1967, many tried to find the treasure they were sure was buried there. Nothing was ever found.

CURSES FROM THE GRAVE

Those who interfere with old monuments or tombs, or who move ancient *standing stones*, often seem to be risking general misfortune, a bad accident or even death. It is as if some places are still *possessed* by the spirits of those who built them or were buried there, or they have become channels for some *supernatural* power working through them.

Tutankhamun's tomb

When the tomb of the Egyptian pharaoh Tutankhamun was found in 1923, it had not been disturbed for thousands of years. It was entered by a party led jointly by the English Lord Carnarvon and a man called Howard Carter.

By 1930, Carter was the only one from that party left alive. Many say that this is just *coincidence* – although there was a warning on the tomb that whoever disturbed it should suffer the *Curse* of the Pharaohs.

Lord Carnarvon had already been warned in a letter from a famous *clairvoyant* not to enter the tomb. Worried, he went to a *palm reader* who gave him the same advice. But Lord Carnarvon decided to ignore this advice and defying the pharaohs went ahead with the expedition. He was one of the first of the party to die, only a few weeks after setting foot inside the tomb. Officially he died from an insect bite, although some claimed that the position of the bite exactly corresponded to a mark on the mask of Tutankhamun.

At the exact moment of Carnarvon's death in Egypt, his dog in England let out a long howl and died.

Cursed objects

Objects which are taken from tombs as souvenirs often carry a deadly curse with them. A diamond, called the Hope Diamond, which had been plundered from the forehead of an Indian idol, seems to have caused death and misfortune to whoever has owned it. One French owner was pulled to pieces by mad dogs, and Marie Antoinette, the last French queen, who owned the diamond for a while, was guillotined during the French Revolution. More recently, a young American woman, Evalyn McLean, who was joint heiress to the diamond, was found dead in mysterious circumstances in her apartment. In

Sir Alexander Seaton and his wife, Zeyla, stole a small human bone from an Egyptian tomb in 1936. Back home in Scotland it was put in a glass cabinet. After that, the room containing the bone was often found in a terrible mess and strange sounds were heard. Occasionally a ghostly figure was seen in the house. One night, during a dinner party, the bone, showcase, and the table it stood on hurtled across the room of their own accord. Although Sir Alexander eventually burnt the *relic*, he was convinced that bad luck followed him all his life because of it.

In Dorset, England, the skull of a black servant boy, who died in the 18th century, is sealed up in Bettiscombe Manor. If any attempt to move the skull is made, terrible disturbances happen and it is said that serious bad luck is brought to the household. The skull has also been known to scream and sweat drops of blood.

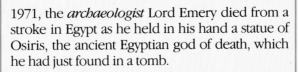

The 'Curse of the Pharaohs' (see main text) came into operation when the Egyptian tomb of Tutankhamun was opened in 1923. It was said to have killed off at least 22 people over the next few years. Lord Carnarvon, the joint leader of the expedition, joked as he entered the tomb although he had been warned of the curse. He died within two months. At the time of his death, all the lights in Cairo went out.

1971, the *archaeologist* Lord Emery died from a stroke in Egypt as he held in his hand a statue of Osiris, the ancient Egyptian god of death, which he had just found in a tomb.

Angry stones

There are many accounts of stones which mysteriously return to their old site if they are moved (see page 7). Others do not move back, but cause all sorts of frightening disturbances. In 1944, some US Air Force men moved a stone in Great Leigh, England, which was supposed to mark a witch's grave. After that, hens stopped laying eggs in the area, cows produced no milk, haystacks mysteriously fell over and church bells rang of their own accord. As soon as the stone was put back where it was, the disturbances stopped.

Animals seem to be particularly sensitive to the 'feelings' of old stones. When a Scottish farmer took a stone from a standing stone circle and built it into a cowshed door, the cows refused to pass underneath it.

It has also been noticed that ancient stones sometimes seem to object to being measured or even touched. In 1740, an English architect called John Wood tried to draw a plan of the Stanton Drew stone circles in Somerset, England. He had to abandon the plan, like others before him, when a violent storm blew up knocking over a huge tree nearby. A similar thing happened when he tried to draw plans of Stonehenge.

Tree curses

There is an old tradition in Japan which forbids the cutting down of trees near any country sanctuary. It is said that in AD 661, the Empress Saimei had all the trees in a sacred grove cut down for her new palace to be built. As soon as it was built, it was destroyed by the elements, and many of the courtiers killed. The same thing happened to a soldier who took the wood for his own use.

After the English Civil War, the king was executed and Oliver Cromwell took over the country. It is said that when he went to live in one of the former king's palaces he cut down an ancient tree called the King's Oak, to burn in the fire. Immediately all sorts of strange things happened. The logs were hurled round the room, ink spilt, ghostly dogs and footsteps were heard and horses' bones appeared from nowhere and were hurled on the company. Cromwell's men fled from the palace in panic.

Early this century, an old farmer on the Orkney Islands, Scotland found an ancient *earthmound* on his land. As he dug it out, a strange wild man appeared, dressed in rags, who warned the farmer that if he did not leave the mound alone, six of his cattle would die and there would be six funerals from his house. The farmer ignored the warning, which came true in every detail.

MIRACLES AND WONDERS

A *miracle* is something which defies all known laws of science – something which really should not be able to happen at all. How can objects made of stone move and even bleed, for instance? Or why should people with incurable diseases or festering wounds suddenly become healed overnight? Although *sceptics* would deny the existence of miracles, they do seem to have occured by the thousand all over the world and since time began.

Many miracles are associated with holy places, or seem to have some religious significance. No one knows why this is so, although devoutly religious people would say it is God's way of communicating with us.

The holy shroud of Turin

The shroud of Turin is a piece of cloth, 4.20 metres long, and 1.05 metres wide. It is made from finely-woven, expensive linen and has the perfect image of a bearded man, front and back, somehow printed on it. The man is dead, and there are wounds on his wrists, feet and chest – and some marks on his body as if he had been whipped. Many believe that the cloth is the shroud used to wrap Christ's body after the crucifixion.

The mystery about the shroud is how the image came to be on the cloth. Some say that it was painted on in the 14th century by a clever forger, and the shroud was then falsely shown as a holy *relic*. Others believe that the image could have been made by a combination of the burial oils used on the body, and sweat. Another theory states that the image was made by the flash of energy given off when Christ came back to life.

Tests are now being carried out to determine the shroud's age. No matter what the results, however, the image on the shroud is miraculous if genuine, and almost equally amazing if it is forged.

Living statues and paintings

Some objects appear to have taken on a life of their own in a most remarkable way. There are many reports of religious icons or paintings moving their eyes, making the sign of the cross with their hands, or even crying or bleeding. In 1920, during an earlier time of great hatred and violence in Ireland, all religious statues and

The ancient Roman poet Ovid recorded how an oak tree, thought to be the home of a spirit called a dryad, gushed a crimson blood-like substance when it was cut down. Other classical writers tell similar stories about statues of gods weeping and sweating.

In 1653, the people sitting in Sacro Monte chapel saw a drunk man come in the door. To their amazement, a stone cockerel on a statue of St Peter began to scold the man loudly and flap its wings. It repeated these actions several times before becoming still again. The drunk man reformed from that day on.

When the shroud of Turin (see main text) is photographed, the outline and features of the bearded man become very clearly-defined on the negative. It has also been possible, with advanced computer techniques, to construct an accurate three-dimensional model of the man's face.

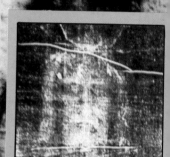

These sections from the photograph have been made into positive images and clearly show the bearded face and crossed hands of the figure.

paintings in the house of Thomas Dwan of Templemore, Tipperaray, began to bleed.

It is not always religious objects which so miraculously come to life. When the Polish composer, Frederick Chopin, died in 1849, a death-mask made of his face was seen to shed tears by several witnesses.

Some say that when people claim to see objects move on their own, they are really practising the ancient art of *scrying*. This is the ability to 'see' images in shiny surfaces and is used, for instance, by fortune-tellers gazing into crystal balls. Some claim that scrying is a much more widespread ability than is usually thought. The ability, however, seems as mysterious as the moving objects themselves.

Stigmata

Sometimes people develop wounds on their body for no apparent reason. Over the years, it has been known for some Christians to develop bleeding wounds similar to those of Christ. This is called the *stigmata*. Some bleed from their hands or feet or from the forehead where the crown of thorns was placed on Christ's head. An Italian monk, Padre Pio, bled continuously from his hands, feet and side for over 50 years.

Many think that the stigmata is unconsciously produced by the mind. There are cases of disturbed or highly emotional people who are able to produce horrific wounds and bruises by thinking about them.

Death immunity

Some people seem to have the most miraculous escapes from death. In 1803, for instance, an Australian man called Joseph Samuels was sentenced to death for murdering a policeman. When they tried to hang him, however, the rope broke in half at the last moment. A second rope then unravelled before Samuels could be hung and a third also broke. After this Samuels, who had always said he was innocent, was pardoned.

Another miraculous escape from death happened in 1881, when the crew of the 'Lara' had to abandon ship in the middle of the Pacific Ocean. The survivors were close to death from lack of water when the captain noticed they had sailed into an area of green water in the middle of the surrounding blue. Tasting it, he realized with amazement that they had found a miraculous oasis of fresh water in the middle of the ocean.

In 1945, on the day the atomic bomb was dropped on the Japanese city of Hiroshima, a bronze bust of a Japanese girl belonging to an American businessman in Pittsburgh, USA, began to shed tears. Later, it was noticed that there were green marks down the statue's face, thought to be caused by a chemical reaction with the tears.

Saint Anthony of Padua, who died in 1231, was well-known for his inspiring preaching. When his coffin was opened 400 years later, it is claimed that Saint Anthony's perfectly preserved pink tongue was found, sitting in the dust of his body.

GLOSSARY

Alchemy The half-scientific, half magical study of how to change base metals into gold, and prolong life.

Aliens Creatures that do not come from this planet. Usually thought to be the occupants of unidentified flying objects.

Angel hair A white thread-like substance that falls from the sky and disintegrates when touched.

Anthropology The study of humans, their origins and social habits.

Apemen An unknown species of animal, half-man and half-ape reported to live in remote areas of the world.

Archaeology The study of human history by finding and digging up remains of human settlements.

Aura Invisible atmosphere surrounding objects or living things.

Ball lightning A rare form of lightning in a ball shape.

Changeling A fairy child left in exchange for a human baby by the fairies.

Clairvoyance The ability to 'see' into the future, using the mind, not the eyes.

Close Encounters Categories of sightings of unidentified flying objects.

Coincidence Events that happen by chance at the same time and appear to be connected.

Comet A star-like object with a tail, seen moving across the sky.

Curse An appeal to a supernatural power for harm to come to a person or a group of people.

Dowsing The ability to detect eg water, hidden underground using a pendulum or dowsing rod.

Earthmounds Ancient mounds of earth built by prehistoric Man, sometimes in elaborate patterns, for an unknown reason.

Ecstasy A feeling of great joy or delight.

Elixir A mixture to be swallowed which is supposed to prolong life indefinitely.

Equinoxes Two occasions six months apart when day and night are of equal length.

Evolution The gradual development of all living things.

Excavate Dig out objects carefully, eg ancient pottery buried in the ground.

Extinct A species that has completely died out of existence.

Fakir Muslim or Hindu holy man.

Fire immunity The capacity to touch fire without being burnt.

Force field An area which has special, invisible properties, or a strong atmosphere.

Fossil The remains of a plant or animal preserved the earth for many years.

Galaxy The entire star system including the sun and planet Earth.

Hallucination Seeing something clearly which is no really there.

Humanoid Having the appearance of being human

Hypnosis When a person is in a sleep-like state bu still able to answer questions and function as if awake.

Hysteria A condition in which a person becomes uncontrollably excited.

Legend A traditional story about a person or even in the past which is popularly believed but not necessarily true.

Levitation Rising off the ground in defiance of gravity.

Ley lines Lines of magnetic force thought to run through the earth.

Luminous Bright, shining, giving off light.

Mass hysteria A crowd in a state of uncontrolled excitement or emotion.

Meditation Concentrating the mind on religious o spiritual things.

Medium Someone who can be used as a go-between or 'telephone line' between this world and the next.

Meteorite A fragment of fallen rock or metal from outer space.

Milky Way A band of light made from millions of stars stretching across the night-sky.

Miracle An amazing event. Something which would normally be thought of as impossible.

Mummify To preserve dead bodies by drying them out and embalming them.

Mind over matter Gaining control over the body or external things through mind power.

Mystic A seeker after religious or spiritual truth.

Neanderthal Man A stone-age ancestor of Man thought to be extinct.

Omen An object or event which seems to herald either some disaster or a piece of good luck.

Orbit The curved path followed by, eg a planet round the sun or a satellite round the earth.

Palm reader One who studies lines on the palms of the hands believing they show character and destiny.

Petrify To turn into stone.

Phenomenon (plural phenomena) An amazing event.

Plesiosaur A sea-serpent thought to be extinct.

Poltergeist A 'noisy ghost', which makes its presence known by acts of mischief eg moving objects.

Possession When a person is thought to have been entered and then taken over by a spirit.

Prehistoric Before recorded history began.

Psychic Sensitive to forces outside the natural laws of science, or someone with this sensitivity.

Psychokinesis (PK) The ability to move objects through mind power.

Psychometry The ability to know the history of an object through touching it.

Radar Electronic device on aeroplanes and ships which shows all large objects within a certain range.

Relic The remains of a person or object from the past.

Seance A meeting during which the spirits of the dead are contacted.

Sceptic A person who is unwilling to believe a certain fact or theory.

Scrying The art of seeing images when gazing into shiny substances, eg a crystal ball.

Solstice In midwinter it is the shortest day of the year and in midsummer, the longest, caused by the position of the sun.

Sonar Machine giving off sound waves which are bounced back by objects in their path. Used for finding objects in, for example, deep and murky water.

Spontaneous human combustion When a person suddenly bursts into flames for no known reason.

Standing stones Big stones set up as monuments thousands of years ago either important in themselves or marking a significant site, the reasons for which are no longer known.

Star jelly A slimy substance, thought to be a type of fungus or insect eggs.

Stigmata Marks on the body corresponding to Christ's wounds in head, hands, feet and side.

Supernatural The existence of magical powers or properties that are believed to be physically impossible in our world.

Telepathy The ability to communicate by thought alone.

Teleportation Travelling in an instant from one place to another without visible means of transport and possibly through time. Thought to be controlled by the mind.

Thought projection The ability to make thoughts become solid images.

Tornado A violent storm of whirling winds, often with a funnel-shaped cloud.

UFO Unidentified flying objects often reported as flying saucers or spaceships and flown by aliens.

UFOlogy The study of unidentified flying objects.

Vision A spontaneous image of something which is not physically there.

Waterspout A whirling column of water and spray formed by whirlwind between sea and clouds.

Yoga A system of exercise and meditation based on Hindu philosophy.

ACKNOWLEDGEMENTS

The publisher has made every effort to trace ownership of all copyrighted photographs and illustrations and to secure permission for their reproduction. In the event of any question arising as to the use of such material the publisher, whilst expressing regret for inadvertent error, will be pleased to make the necessary corrections in future printings. Thanks are due to the following for permission to use the material indicated.

7　Irish cottage, photo Colin Smythe Ltd
12　UFO flying between the earth and moon, photo Major Ret. Colman S. VonKeviczky, ICUFON
16　Satellite picture taken over the North Pole, photo NASA
24　Strange footprint in the Himlayan Mountains, photo top left, Royal Geographical Society
　　Female Bigfoot at Bluff Creek, photo bottom left, Rene Dahinden, Fortean Picture Library
28　The Loch Ness Monster, photo R K Wilson, Fortean Picture Library
29　The Loch Ness Monster, photo bottom left, Express Newspapers
　　The Loch Ness Monster, photo top right, Anthony Shiels, Fortean Picture Library

30　Kuda Bux firewalking, photo Harry Price Library
31　Ahmed Hussein after a firewalk, photo Mary Evans Picture Library
32　Subbayah Pullavar levitates, photo Mary Evans Picture Library
35　Dean Liddell, Rector of Christchurch Cathedral, Oxford and image on cathedral wall, photos Fortean Picture Library
36　Fallen trees in Tuguska's meteorite area, photo Tass
44　Shroud of Turin, photo BBC Hulton Picture Library

Index

William Collins Sons & Co Ltd
London · Glasgow · Sydney · Auckland
Toronto · Johannesburg

First Published in Great Britain 1989
© William Collins Sons & Co Ltd

Printed in Great Britain by
BPCC Paulton Books Limited

Beasant, Pam
World mysteries.
1. Mysteries – For children
I. Title II. Miller, Tony
001.9'4
ISBN 0-00-190021-X
ISBN 0-00-190069-2 Pbk